Glowing Reviews

for Christian Heath and Love the SAT! Test Prep from Students and Parents:

"Christian, Thomas came home last night and said (about you) 'He is a great teacher, he gets me and doesn't judge me and he doesn't make me feel stupid.' Thank you so much!!" R. *(a mom)*

"Just a short note to tell you WHAT a FABULOUS job that you are doing with the class. Luke has really appreciated your teaching manner & not complained about going! WOW – credit to you! Best, J." *(a mom)*

"He seems to like the class and describes you as the 'Mr. Miyagi' of the SAT... C." *(a dad)*

"By the way, thank you for the added bonus of guiding Alia in her future. She said you were an excellent SAT teacher, but more importantly a remarkable life coach! ;-))" - J. *(a mom)*

"I had researched SAT prep courses and came across Christians information. I started emailing him a year prior to using him. His follow up is exceptional and he was very informative in his information that he provided via email. . I bought the book he recommended and coauthored and had my daughter start studying prior to her one on one sessions. She LOVED working with Christian. He worked at her level and moved at her pace. She looked forward to going to class. I would HIGHLY recommend the Love the SAT classes and will be sending my other daughter their next year." - K. *(a mom)*

"Boaz was very happy to have attended your class. I know that he doesn't always express his feelings, but attending your class definitely made him more confident and excited about the SAT. I have told a number of family and friends about your class and will continue to spread the word. Thanks again for taking the time to tutor Bo, I am grateful, C." *(a mom)*

("A Teacher Who Changed Your Life" - by one of my students from China)

"I didn't like to memorize things. I hated to memorize things. I thought i wasn't good at memorizing things. Until I took a SAT course in the summer. I met a teacher, his name was Christian. He always smiled, every time had a happy look in his face. He was also really energetic, he went from one side to the other side of the classroom.

First day of summer school. He taught us about the basics of a SAT course. He made a pyramid and on the bottom there was motivation. He told us that motivation was the most important thing that students needed.

Those words just struck in my mind. I wasn't even close to the top of the pyramid. I figured out that I didn't have any motivation. I thought about my life after school. The first thing that I do when I go back to home is watching a television show. Even from this I could feel that I didn't have motivation.

Throughout the summer school. Everysingle class Christian told us that we need to have motivation in order to be good at anything in this world. After hearing these words for a week. I finally got some motivation. I closed everything, every electronic device that would bother me. I spent just 20 minutes everyday after school memorizing vocabs.

After few months I figured out that I had learned more then 500 words perfectly. I realized that it wasn't me who was bad at memorizing things. It was myself who didn't have motivation to do things. I was going the easy, lazy way.

"Although it was a short time being with Christian, I had learn alot of things from him. He was the engine that started me to get going. If i meet him again I really want to thank him. I wish i could eventually meet him again."

- Anonymous student, Chengdu, China

"I've spoken at length with Christian about the SAT and his philosophy toward tutoring and test prep. I've always been very impressed with his insights and approach to instruction.

"As a test prep professional myself, I meet a lot of charismatic people who sell their personality over substance or emphasize fake tricks and tips over real learning. I've never suspected Christian of falling into this camp. He's a highly motivated educator, who cares about his students and works diligently to help them succeed. If you're in need of test prep, I highly recommend you give him a call."

- Matt McCorkle, Co-Founder: Clear Choice Test Prep

Contact Us

Our entire reason to exist as a tutoring and publishing company is simply to help you succeed.

We work primarily with 9th-12th graders who are headed on to great things for college and career... OR who simply want to make it to university.

We are always available if you just shoot a quick email to Help@LovetheSAT.com.

Please contact us today (or any time!) for assistance and advice on:

- SAT Prep
- ACT Prep
- PSAT Prep
- College Counseling
- College Applications
- College Essays
- Scholarship Advising

Find us on the Web and Social Media:

- www.LovetheSAT.com
- www.Facebook.com/LovetheSAT
- Twitter: @LovetheSAT
- Email: Help@LovetheSAT.com

For More Great Lessons from Christian Heath and Love the SAT Test Prep:

Complete Online Courses for Teens:

- Ultimate Time Management for Teens and Students
  (Get the complete course on discount just for you!)
  - https://www.udemy.com/ultimate-time-management-for-teens-and-high-school-students/?couponCode=TimeBookCompleteCourse

- Conquer SAT Vocabulary for Higher Reading and Verbal Scores
  - https://www.udemy.com/conquer-sat-vocabulary/?couponCode=TimeManagementBook

- Winning College Scholarships for High Schoolers
  - https://www.udemy.com/winning-college-scholarships/?couponCode=TimeBookScholarship

Print Books and eBooks:

Look for them on Amazon.com and LovetheSAT.com!

- SAT Grammar Crammer

- (Coming Soon) Top 30 Incredible Examples for High School Essay Evidence

Free Articles and Blogs:
- www.LovetheSAT.com/blog
- www.eSATPrepTips.com/articles

On Social Media:
- www.Facebook.com/LovetheSAT
- Twitter: @LovetheSAT
- Find us on YouTube!

Web, Email and Phone:
- www.LovetheSAT.com/contact_us
- Help@LovetheSAT.com
- 1-800-653-8994

Ultimate Time Management
for Teens and Students

Join the Class on Facebook!

Throughout this book you will find prompts to leave a quick post on our Facebook wall (www.Facebook.com/LovetheSAT)

Please take advantage of EVERY opportunity to do so!

This end-of-chapter activity is designed to increase your engagement, help you learn, and to work as a class.

Prove to yourself that you can defeat procrastination with action. Join the rest of the class for a discussion on the Facebook page after you finish reading each chapter and quiz!

Don't be shy! We're all here to learn (including me!)

Come introduce yourself today – at www.Facebook.com/LovetheSAT.

- Christian

Ultimate
Time Management
for
Teens and Students

Become massively more productive in high school with powerful lessons from a pro SAT tutor and top-10 college graduate.

By Christian Heath

Love the SAT Academic Press

Dedicated to my students in the U.S. and China.

CONTENTS

CONTENTS

ACKNOWLEDGMENTS

This book would not have been possible without the support of the Love the SAT team – especially Christopher Bakka and Michael Webbon, who held the fort while I wrote the manuscript.

I also owe a great debt to Napoleon Hill, from whom I have learned so much about setting goals and getting my work done. And thanks again to all my students past and present for the lessons you've taught me.

"Better three hours too soon than a minute too late."

- William Shakespeare

"Time is a sort of river of passing events, and strong is its current; no sooner is a thing brought to sight than it is swept by and another takes its place, and this too will be swept away."

- Marcus Aurelius, Emperor of Rome 161-180 AD

READ THIS FIRST

Welcome to <u>Ultimate Time Management for Teens and Students</u> from **Christian Heath** (that's me) and **Love the SAT Test Prep** (that's my company)!

Consider this page a short introduction and "easy-start guide" to this book for teens and high schoolers.

I've kept the chapters of the book organized by topic, so you *can* skip around the various chapters, but I think the *best* experience comes from reading front-to-back.

You also are holding a book that's filled with interactive moments, like our "class" discussion board on Facebook and the comprehension quizzes throughout the chapters.

Several of the most important chapters also have **"Additional Readings"** attached with a link to a blog article at the end. Please read these additional articles at your convenience.

Use these interactive elements to increase your engagement, which helps you notice and remember more – which saves you time in the long run.

Please **take notes** while you read the book. As you will learn, this simple practice will eventually save you hundreds of hours throughout your life.

These lessons are intended to help from age 14 to age 100 – they will help you for the rest of your life, if you open your mind and heart to them.

Final note – Please get in touch! Ask me any questions at any time! You should use the Facebook wall (<u>www.Facebook.com/LovetheSAT</u>) as well as our main email (<u>Help@LovetheSAT.com</u>) to ask me anything or just to say hello.

And now, without further ado...

1. MEET YOUR INSTRUCTOR

Hello, and welcome to "Ultimate Time Management for Teens and Students" from Love the SAT!

I'm Christian Heath, the founder of Love the SAT Test Prep as well as the founding author of the blog and website eSAT Prep Tips.com.

For the past six years, I've been focused full-time on solving the problems of high school students and their parents as they attempt to make the leap from high school to college.

Although you might be able to tell from our company name that we *originally* focused exclusively on SAT and ACT prep, I eventually realized that high school students everywhere share a barrage of challenges.

And one of the *greatest* of those challenges is finding the TIME to get everything done in your busy life.

So, in order to make our SAT and ACT lessons more effective, we've also broadened our focus and expanded our lesson plans, books, and book offerings specifically to help teenagers and high schoolers in ways that reach far beyond the dry and academic lessons of test prep -

We wanted to help high schoolers EVERYWHERE deal with AGE-OLD problems of going from being a KID to being a YOUNG ADULT...

And that's where we came up with the idea for books and books just like this one on Time Management.

Now, before we get started, I'd like to tell you a little bit more about myself.

That way you can get to know me a little better as an instructor and really so that you can learn why it's gonna be worth hearing me out and listening to what I have to teach you and discuss with you.

So, let's back it up over a DECADE to my years in high school - it actually seems almost just like yesterday.

In High School I was a strong student - I took the hardest classes my school offered in math and science, I mostly stayed on honor roll, took some fun electives and played at least one season of varsity sports per year, plus I was usually part of the outdoor club on the off-seasons from lacrosse.

I also played guitar and keyboard in a band with my friends, studied a bit of classical piano, hung out with friends and played video games pretty much like a lot of people do these days, and I also really liked to read, as long as it was a book I liked.

Just LISTING the stuff I used to do reminds me that one of the most memorable things about high school, for me, was how *INSANELY* busy I always was -

Either running around non-stop or sitting at my desk pounding out homework assignments or freaking out about tomorrow's big test that I felt like I hadn't been given enough time to study for.

To be honest, my time-management skills weren't that great and I relied a lot on my parents to keep me organized, and my teachers to stretch the deadlines for me, which constantly led to tension, frustration and a feeling of cramming at the last minute to make the deadline... again.

Yet, on sheer effort and energy along, and hopefully a few brains rattling around in my head, somehow I got through it all and got into Pomona College, in sunny Claremont California - a school that's regularly rated in the top 10 and often even the top 3 private liberal arts colleges in the United States, which is pretty cool in terms of bragging rights.

When I got to college, I experienced the typical Freshman year uncertainties...

But, I settled down relatively quickly into my chosen field of study, which started off as medicine trying to become a doctor - but the truth is I didn't really like it at all.

One thing I've always been LUCKY to have is a pretty strong sense that I should do what I feel is RIGHT, so by the end of the year I chose to follow my passion at the time of classical music and live piano performance and composition.

One of the best things I learned in college from this experience is that when you're pursuing something you *love* (and for me it was music), it's SO much easier to keep up the discipline to set yourself on a rigorous schedule and keep to it and actually be HAPPY about it.

For example, the more I enjoyed the piano piece I was learning at the moment, the more I would cut short meals, skip time-wasting social events I didn't really care about, and generally avoid wasting time BECAUSE I craved the feeling of working towards my musical goals which I cared SO much about!

So by sophomore year of college, I was LEADING and ORGANIZING some musical groups, taking part in others on the piano, I was working on independent solo projects in performance and composition, while also studying, writing essays, and being tested upon several hundred years of music history - which takes TONS of reading, trust me -

And I was at least *attempting* to remain social with my friends and family - and maintain my health - and have some fun – *and* get some sleep (although that last one didn't really happen too much of the time!).

Basically in college, I stepped up my time management game significantly, although I didn't really think about it in those terms at the time, because I had accidentally unlocked one of the major keys of time management:

Basically, you're going to be NATURALLY much better at smart time management when you both care about AND enjoy the projects you're working on.

Now, that fortunate lesson was not lost on me after I graduated from college...

But it took almost TWO YEARS for me to mentally adjust and make the shift to the so-called "real world" and having a normal job because at first I found it VERY DIFFICULT to be a part of work that I truly cared about.

Part of that is DEFINITELY because in most cases, right out of college people get entry-level jobs with entry-level work and after the challenges of college it's not always exciting and can actually be pretty BORING, unfortunately.

Well, that's basically what happened to me - I got super bored, super quick.

But since college had been SO challenging and SO exciting for me, it was VERY difficult to focus on the new working world and my well-developed time-management skills absolutely CRUMBLED.

And for the FIRST time in my life, EVER, I found myself wasting HUGE amounts of time because I didn't really have any focus guiding my schedule and I didn't really care for what I was working on.

If you're taking this book, that might be sort of similar to some of your OWN problems right now.

Well, because I really wanted an actual challenge again that actually made me feel ALIVE and ENGAGED, I set off to start my own business.

... And BELIEVE me when I say that demanded a HUGE step up from me in terms of personal time management and still does on an ongoing basis.

The business I chose to start was an SAT and ACT prep tutoring company called "Love the SAT" and then I also added a second blog called eSAT Prep Tips.com.

While I was building the basics of these businesses, I found out that I really enjoyed teaching and the fun of working with high school students on the most challenging of material.

And, now that the BUSINESS to be a focus in my life that I cared about as much as I cared about MUSIC in COLLEGE, I now had a reason again to put in the effort to take control of my schedule bit by bit.

Now, after five years of running the business full time, my time-management and personal discipline skills are sharper than ever, but I didn't reach this point overnight.

It's taken a LOT of trial and error, back and forth, push and pull for me to get to the level I'm at NOW and I feel like there are MANY higher levels above this that I can keep striving to reach.

But, it's also good to celebrate our progress and like I said, I want to introduce myself and my qualifications, as well as reassure you that I really do know what I'm talking about, because it's always easier to relax and learn when you TRUST your teacher.

So, let's take a quick trip through the highlights of our company's progress so far:

- I've worked with over five hundred high school students just like you - each of them at a different natural level of academic achievement and personal time management

- I'm the author of six books for high schoolers and parents on topics from essay-writing to SAT math, available on Amazon, with more on the way.

- Despite the fact that I live and work in the center of Texas in the United States, I was personally invited - TWICE - to teach SAT prep to high schoolers in China at a prestigious international school there.

- That might have something to do with the fact that the average rating of our tutoring company, Love the SAT, is 4.6 out of 5 stars from students and parents after being in business for 5 years.

- And, in our most recent and most exciting expansion yet, we've created and released multiple online books like this one to help students like you in the realms of test prep as well as MANY other important skills for high school, college, and career.

Since the day I founded our company in 2011, I've been thinking about new ways to help more students around the world, and creating awesome new online books is one of my favorite ideas ever.

As you can maybe tell, my life depends on juggling a lot of different demands - probably just like YOURS does.

Without the skills of time management that I've developed over the tough years of high school, I probably wouldn't have gotten into college.

Without my time in COLLEGE, I'm pretty sure my business would fail, and I would definitely be a MUCH worse musician.

And, if I can't control my time, I'm also never able to hang out with friends and family and that's not good.

So to me, "time management" isn't some abstract idea - it's an important daily tool that allows me to continue my happy life un-interrupted, and it's something that I use to help my students succeed in our classes and tutoring sessions.

As long as there are just 24 hours in a day, we'll all continue to struggle with our priorities and time management, our scheduling and our deadlines -

As long as I'm HUMAN and not a robot, I expect that I will need to learn how to manage my time effectively.

So, that's a bit about me that I hope helps you understand WHO I am and WHY I'm so excited to be writing the Ultimate Course on Time Management for Teens.

Based on my experiences with high-level academics, my years of private tutoring and teaching with high school students, plus a decade of self-directed, self-scheduled work in entrepreneurship and music performance -

Well, basically all that made me a *natural* to create this book on Time Management and I'm really excited that we're both a part of it.

Now, just to be fair, I want YOU to introduce yourself.

Take a moment to pause before the next chapter and use our Facebook page (www.Facebook.com/LovetheSAT) to let me know your NAME, whether you're a PARENT or a STUDENT, your year in high school, and your current biggest time-management problem in life.

I want you to make sure you do this because I'm going to have many more questions for you throughout the book and I want you to get in the habit of answering them in a semi-public forum -

Not only is this a form of practice to eliminate procrastination, it's also going to help you stay FOCUSED and ENGAGED with this book...

Which is GREAT, because I'll tell you that after being a full-time top student and then a full-time top teacher for 20 plus years I can PROMISE you that if you GIVE more engagement in class you will GET so much more out of the experience, which *in itself* is a way of maximizing your limited time.

Also, if everyone reading the book CONTRIBUTES to the discussions we'll all get access to an awesome forum of extra bonus info that we can all read to find out more about what other people are struggling with and how they're improving their time-management skills right alongside you.

So start your good habits right now and put down the book for a moment to visit our Facebook page (www.Facebook.com/LovetheSAT) and leave your name, whether you're a parent or student, your current grade or year in high school, and your biggest time management problem that you face, and I'll see you in the next chapter!

2. OVERVIEW OF THIS BOOK

So, now that you know a little about me and why I've developed my OWN time management principles to work with, let's talk about the structure of this book.

The **first major section** of this book (Chapters 3-10) leads off with timeless time management principles that will work for anyone.

I thought that was important to begin with, because not only does it give us a solid foundation of time management skills for any age and any situation, it ALSO gives us a framework of ideas, terms, and definitions to use for the SECOND section of the book, which is focused entirely on time management for teenagers and high schoolers.

By starting off with timeless ideas, it helps lay the foundation to apply the general principles of the good time management to the specific demands placed on high school teenagers.

In the **second and largest section** (Chapters 11-29), that's where we look at specific approaches to scheduling, organization and time management that are really going to resonate with you as a student or parent because the tips are focused around the EXACT daily, weekly and yearly goals and demands of being a teenager in high school.

Then, the **final section** (Chapters 30-32) is an efficient review of what we've covered to help you review and organize your notes and retain what you've learned.

Certain chapters will have additional reading materials attached in the form of **a hyperlink** to bonus articles that I'd like you to read on our blog.

It's all aimed at HELPING you increase your engagement, increase your recall and save you time in the long run -

Basically, taking the time to complete all the extra reading makes this book, and the *time* you spend on it, a better investment for YOU.

Speaking of engagement, recall, and return on investment, please be SURE to take written or typed notes as you go through the book!

One of the classic principles of good time management is that taking notes isn't just to give you something to look at later..

It's also the very ACT of TAKING notes that increases your memory and REDUCES the amount of review study you need.

End result? Taking notes actually INCREASES your free time - it just doesn't always FEEL like it while you're taking them.

I encourage you take the next step in your maturity as a student and lifelong learner, BUST out the pen and paper and start taking notes right now if you haven't already.

Also, please share the name of this book with your friends and peers as you go, so you can all discuss the concepts and become more efficient together!

If you ever have a question for me, use the Facebook page (www.Facebook.com/LovetheSAT) to ask it in a forum-style setting that the other students and I can see and respond to!

I will DEFINITELY respond to your question and I'm always glad when students show me some curiosity because that's a sign I'm getting through to you.

So never feel shy about speaking up and asking me anything you want to know, and it will ALSO probably help at least ten other people who were wondering the exact same thing but were too shy to ask it.

If you have a PRIVATE question, you can also contact me via email (Help@LovetheSAT.com) or through our website (www.LovetheSAT.com).

Now, I want you to start practicing your own time management skills right away.

Set a "finish date" for this book - a deadline that YOU are giving yourself to complete 100% of the book, exercises, and additional reading.

Then work backwards from the deadline to today. How long do you have, and how much progress do you need to make each day?

Now, add it to your calendar to make the commitment!

Then please SHARE your start date and your DEADLINE for completion on the Facebook page (www.Facebook.com/LovetheSAT).

I think it will help us ALL if we pause our reading right now and SHARE our intended date of completion for the book on the Facebook page.

Finally, make sure to go to Amazon.com and leave me a review on the book and some honest feedback, either while you read or at the end of the book.

It really makes a LOT of difference to me to know what you think of the book.

Now - I'm excited to get started with our lessons on timeless time management principles.

These lessons will help you win scholarships, get into the most popular colleges, ace your classes with less effort, and really, do anything you want in life.

Don't forget to share your deadline with me on our Facebook page and I'll meet you in the next chapter!

QUIZ #1: REVIEW OF THE INTRODUCTION

Welcome to the first quiz of Ultimate Time Management for Teens and Students!

The idea behind these quizzes is that they give you an extra reason to pay attention and to check your memory.

There's no time limit. Go slowly and try to get them all correct.

Answers are on page 187.

QUESTION #1: What is MY name (the author's name / your instructor?)

A) Christopher Kaplan
B) Christian Heath
C) Chewbacca
D) Mike McCormick

QUESTION #2: What is the name of our tutoring company?

A) Test-Takers Anonymous
B) SAT PrepMasters
C) Love the SAT Test Prep
D) Ultimate Tutoring Inc.

QUESTION #3: What's the name of the book you're currently reading?

A) Timely Time Management for High School
B) Time for More Time in School
C) Ultimate Time Management for Teens and Students

QUESTION #4: Who is this book written PRIMARILY for?

A) Busy and stressed high school students who want to go to good colleges!
B) College students who want to remember what high school was like.
C) Parents of high school students.

QUESTION #5: Why should you take notes while you read this book?

A) Notes will help you prove to your parents and teachers that you've done the work that was assigned.
B) Note-taking will make you a faster writer and help you improve your handwriting with every class you take.
C) Notes help you improve your memory and recall - ultimately saving you time in the long run. Plus, you NEED to get good at taking notes in preparation for college.
D) Actually, I said that notes are NOT important - in fact, they're a tremendous waste of your time.

QUESTION #6: Where can you ask your questions about the book?

A) By email (Help@LovetheSAT.com).
B) Our Facebook page (www.Facebook.com/LovetheSAT)
C) The contact form on our website (www.LovetheSAT.com/contact_us)
D) All of the above!

QUESTION #7: Have you set a deadline for completing the book and shared it on the Facebook page (www.Facebook.com/LovetheSAT)?

A) Yes, I've set a deadline and shared it!
B) I've set a deadline, but not shared it.
C) I haven't set a deadline for completing the book.

ANSWERS p.187

3. THE TOP 3 TIMELESS RULES OF TIME MANAGEMENT

Welcome to the first major section of Ultimate Time Management for High Schoolers

Now, this whole book is gonna be specifically about YOU and the needs and demands faced by busy high school students and teenagers.

BUT - I wanted to start off with a section to lay the ground rules of good time management that work at ANY age for ANYONE.

Then when we go on to focus on high school in particular, we'll already be thinking about strategies that make the most of ANY situation, ANY schedule and ANY amount of time.

High school will just be the ENVIRONMENT that we're applying those strategies to.

So, I want to start with my top 3 timeless tips of time management.

Time-management is a personal subject because we all have different goals, rhythms, energy levels, and work schedules.

Each of us will have our own particular twist to getting things done, so it might *seem* hard to uncover any rules that fit EVERYONE.

But it IS possible - if those rules ACKNOWLEDGE the fact that we are all INDIVIDUALS.

That's why each of my top three rules is based around YOU and only you.

Here are the rules:

Rule #1. Know what you want to DO with your life.

Rule #2. Know yourself and your own personal productivity rhythms.

Rule #3. BALANCE is everything. Know what YOU need to stay balanced.

Now, my number-one rule for time management is "Know what you want to DO with your life."

One of the biggest questions we all face is what to work TOWARDS.

What goals and objectives and standards do we set, and how do we measure our progress towards them?

When done right, setting goals gets you excited and that excitement is what keeps you on the path through the hard parts.

Besides, just consider the alternative - which is having no goals in life!

You know that old, cliched saying about "If you don't know where you're trying to go, you'll never get there?"

It's definitely the truth.

In any journey, ESPECIALLY our longest journey - which is the journey of our whole lives - you must set a destination point or there's simply no way to stay on course.

You won't even HAVE a course!

My SECOND rule of time management is to know YOURSELF.

Most importantly for our purposes, you need to understand your own personal rhythms.

We all have strong and weak points during each day, each week, and each year - but there ARE usually recurring patterns to our highs and lows.

So, one key rule to time management at ANY age is to KNOW your current personal rhythms, which can change over the years as your personality changes and your lifestyle changes.

Generally it's almost ALWAYS a good idea to position your need to get stuff DONE around your highest levels of energy during the day.

We'll talk more about this as we go one, but one great way to get started is to keep a SUPER-easy and minimal daily journal to document your goals, productivity, and results at the end of each day.

And a bit more on rule number three: BALANCE is everything.
It's true, balance is everything when it comes to working your hardest and believe it or not, some RELAXING is required for producing at your top potential.

Downtime, and sleep, food, and time for family and friends, is MANDATORY, not optional.

If you're having trouble relaxing, just try considering it part of your JOB description to relax a little every day or you will fail later on when you burn out in the near future.

Be patient. Nothing great is every forced out in a day or even a week or a month.

Greatness takes YEARS of daily effort, and even GOOD results in anything that really matters generally take patience and long-term daily effort.

If it was EASY, everyone else would do it. Now THERE'S a cliche that's 100% true.

So those are my three timeless rules of time management as a framework to our future conversations.

In the next chapter we'll cover how to identify your OWN top one to five priorities in life so you can get the high-level clarity you need to take charge of your schedule and work on the things that really matter to you.

Before you go, head to the Facebook page (www.Facebook.com/LovetheSAT) and leave YOUR personal thoughts on rule number-one:

"Know what you want to DO with your life."

Do YOU have an answer for this question yet?

Or, are you still COMPLETELY unsure... or somewhere in between?

No matter where you stand, head to Facebook to leave your answer, and I'll see you in the next chapter!

4. HOW TO IDENTIFY YOUR TOP 1-5 PRIORITIES IN LIFE

Ok, this next chapter was actually one of the TOUGHEST for me to write, and I've worked on it a lot because there's so much I want to say but I don't want to waste your time and ramble on a topic that's very important to me.

But, I think it's one of THE MOST important chapters of the whole book.

This chapter is about HOW to identify the top one to five things that matter most to you and WHY this matters so much to time management, plus a little background information about my own story so far and my OWN experience trying to figure out WHY I think I'm alive, and how I think it all relates.

See, something I've noticed as I've gotten a little older is that the people with the most FOCUS and CLARITY about their PRIORITIES life are ALSO the ones who are seem to be doing absolutely EXCELLENT and feeling HAPPY and FULFILLED with life.

This focus seems like it can be anything - any focus at all - from their KIDS to their JOBS to their HOBBIES or whatever.

But the trend I see is that HAPPY people are focused on SOMETHING.

Some of us have trouble narrowing down to just ONE thing, we have more like four or five things, but the point is to be very CLEAR about what are your "favorite" things out of ALL the millions of options there are in life.

For me it's business, motorcycles, and music, along with my friends and my health.

These are people, activities, and things that I LOVE to spend time with -

And what's REALLY cool is I feel sure that they are all things that I *really* love, and NOT just things I'm spending time on because my parents, my teachers, or my society told me I had to.

On the other hand, I know PLENTY of people who are NOT happy with their lives and something I've noticed is many times they don't seem to know what they WANT out of life.

OR they have never taken the time and space to figure out what THEY want in life, which means that no matter HOW hard they work, they're probably chasing somebody else's dream - maybe chasing their PARENT's dream or their BOSS's dream or their teachers' dreams.

Since they don't know what they really want deep down, it's impossible to make any PROGRESS towards that goal -

And it's the life equivalent of just paddling in the middle of the ocean with no horizon visible anywhere, no land, no compass and just getting more and more tired of working and swimming without any true sense of direction.

I think, and this is just my personal theory, that having just ONE lifelong focus is the ideal for maximizing productivity and achieving a sense of "flow" and focus in your life, but personally, I'm definitely I'm not there yet.

I've reduced down to about FIVE major spheres of my life that I choose to focus MOST on.

And in fact, it took me until I was about 25 years old to figure out enough about myself to narrow down even to FIVE things - I'm not someone who knew from a super-young age exactly what ONE thing he wanted to do.

I've gone through a LOT of different things over the years to discover what I really care about.

So, I'm not someone who can just put down ONE bullet point that I care about, and then focus all my hours, days, and years around that single goal.

And in some ways I'm a little envious of people who are THAT laser-focused in life, because they accomplish some really cool things early on in life...

BUT the fact that I can say my top five priorities to myself is EXTREMELY helpful when it comes to budgeting my limited time and energy.

See, even though I'm saying it seems best to have ONE true passion in life to focus around, it still might just be IMPOSSIBLE for some personality types like me to narrow down to ONE focus and one focus only.

Basically, I'm contradicting myself a little bit.

Although my personal THEORY is that ONE SINGLE FOCUS is generally best for time management, STILL, I'm living, breathing proof - at least to myself - that it's possible to be pretty good about managing your time as long as your STREAMLINE and SIMPLIFY your main goals.

17

Instead of 10 desires, focus on 5. Instead of 5 desires, focus on 3. Instead of 2 desires, focus on 1.

This simple trick alone is one of the most effective time management concepts you could ever imagine.

That clarity is exactly what gives me the POWER to juggle multiple competing priorities: from managing a business that I started myself, to getting better at guitar and piano, to becoming a better motorcyclist but still not feeling too overburdened or too busy.

Now if you can't narrow down to a single dominating priority, it's also incredibly important to know the RANKING or ORDER of those priorities because this will still bring you to a new level of clarity in your time budgeting.

In terms of my own top five, I know that my personal health comes before everything, because if I'm not HEALTHY I can't do ANYTHING.

It's like those oxygen masks in airplanes - they say to put YOURS on before helping others - because you HAVE to be able to BREATH before you can help.

So, personal physical and mental health always comes first.

Family and friends after that if they are having an EMERGENCY, then business comes next because without my business I will lose my livelihood and that would be very bad.

So a family emergency has priority, but GENERALLY my business has priority over family and friends because if my business fails, I'll be stressed and have no time or money to spend with ANYONE.

After business comes family and friends in all other situations, like just hanging out or watching a movie, and on a fairly even level, we also have motorcycling and music which are my favorite personal hobbies.

These last three are pretty even in terms of my personal rankings, so sometimes I'll waste time not deciding: should I practice guitar? should I work on my motorcycle? should socialize and I call my friends or family?

So, I still have plenty of room to improve.

It would be even BETTER if I got MORE clear about items three through five on my priority list because I could organize my plans better and spend less time and energy "deciding" every single time between music, friends, and motorcycling.

On the other hand, it's nice to include an element of choice and flexibility in my priorities, so maybe it's not such a bad thing - ESPECIALLY since I'm very, very clear on the essential "top 3" things and their rankings.

One is my health. Two is family/friend emergencies. Three is business. After those things, come the fun stuff.

Even this VERY simple ranking structure helps me speed along a busy day or busy week by organizing my competing tasks without too much thought.

In fact, the simplicity of my top-five list IS what makes it effective.

Your days, weeks, and months are COMPLICATED - so while you're in the thick of them, you need a SIMPLE priority list that *comes from your heart* to keep yourself organized.

This is just as true in high school as it is in college and then adult life and the working world.

Never make a priority list that you think OTHER people will approve of.

There are multiple types of people with huge varieties in their personal goals and many of them will try to influence you in YOUR choice of goals -

It's important to listen to your SELF and give yourself plenty of time and personal space to do this research on yourself to find out what you care most about.

Now, what methods can you use to identify your own top priorities?

Here are a few of my favorite ways for myself and for students. Many of them take the form of open-ended questions.

After each question or prompt, please pause in your reading, take out your pen and paper, and spend at least sixty seconds minutes brainstorming and writing down your ideas.

You don't have to come to any conclusions today, but you DO need to start thinking and taking notes.

Question number one is "What do you daydream about?"

This one is simple - pay attention to what you've been thinking about the past few days, weeks, or months.

What do your thoughts keep returning to? Is it a vacation, a sports accomplishment, a fear, a boyfriend or girlfriend?

Use this is as a clue pointing towards your natural, personal top priorities and spend some time thinking about the hidden personality traits your daydreams reveal.

The next question is, "what puts you in FLOW?"

"Flow" is the state of feeling wrapped-up in what you're doing - it's like a mix of focus, excitement, fun, and challenge.

For me, MOTORCYCLING and MUSIC are by FAR the two easiest and most fun ways for me to be in a state of flow for HOURS.

And, it's no coincidence at ALL that music and motorcycling, two of my favorite "flow state" activities, are also two of my top priorities in life.

The cool thing about FLOW is that you can be completely honest with yourself - what do you REALLY get involved in?

Remember to pause and do some personal brainstorming and note-taking on each of these suggestions as you read this chapter!

The next concept to brainstorm around is: Who are your HEROS - who INSPIRES you?

This can be FICTIONAL CHARACTERS and REAL PEOPLE

I have many heroes! From the composer Ludwig van Beethoven to the great motorcycle racer Valentino Rossi, there are many real and imaginary characters who I look up to.

Each of them tells me something about MYSELF -

Beethoven reminds me of the creative, artistic, and challenging side of life; Valentino Rossi reminds me of adventure, danger, and riding skill - and so on and so forth.

By knowing my own heros, I know more about my own values and priorities - and that helps me decide how to manage my time and my life in a way that I find satisfying, fun, personal, and fulfilling.

Take some time now to pause and brainstorm a short list of your favorite idols, heroes, and heroines, then spend a few more minutes trying to figure out exactly what it is about each of them that appeals to you.

Finally, think about how this new info could help you organize your personal life priorities.

Here's another really fun and cool thought I came up with that's a little bit off the beaten path but will help uncover your deepest dreams and goals: what PILGRIMAGES do you want to make?

By "pilgrimages" I mean - special trips to specific places, not just taking a random vacation just anywhere for fun, but specific travel with a PURPOSE.

For example, if you love rock-climbing, then is there a world-famous mountain you'd like to climb, or national park to visit?

If you're a baseball fanatic, do you want to see the Hall of Fame in person?

As a motorcyclist, I maintain a list of places, trips, and specific roads I want to ride in the future.

Desert adventures, challenging mountain roads, and international travel - it's all on the list.

Can you see how this tells me a TON about myself and my priorities?

Rather than wanting to just ride on down to the mall or cafe, I really want to get OUT there and challenge myself with huge, ambitious, difficult motorcycle pilgrimages.

Another example was when I visited Beethoven's grave in Vienna.

Although it was a difficult and cold trip to visit the site on my own, in a country far from home and a language I did not speak, the amount of chillbumps and the nearly religious feeling I got from the experience confirmed that Beethoven's music is especially important to me!

Take some time to pause and think about the top three to five places you'd like to visit, or pilgrimages you'd like to make.

What do those places tell you about yourself and your priorities and values ?

Part of finding your passions and priorities is coming at the question from as many angles as possible.

The next topic I want you to brainstorm and think about is: what sort of specific SKILLS do you want to use day-to-day?

In other words, what do you want to get BETTER at? This can be abstract, like "I want to develop more self-control," or concrete, like "I want to become a pro surfer."

Be sure to think about the LONG TERM of that skill - what is it LIKE to be great at that skill?

Does it have a daily usefulness, or is it more of a niche skill?

Since our time in life is limited, it's always nice to develop skills that have a wide application -

For example, although surfing is a very niche skill, it also develops your physical health, balance, and coordination.

Meanwhile, and nothing against stamp-collecting, but stamp-collecting is probably going to have fewer benefits to your life and might not be quite as rewarding overall as a skill that has more overall benefits and daily uses.

Then again, you could learn all sorts of skills like organizing, researching, history, networking and communication since you're reaching out to stamp clubs, you could start a stamp website, et cetera -

All stuff that could come back in your life or career.

So I take it back - stamp collecting probably teaches you TONS of skills!

Now pause the video and think about what skills you want to be really GOOD at.

This can help you discover your priorities and uncover what you want to DO with your life.

By now you should have a TON of ideas - possibly several pages of ideas and brainstorms - which is what you want!

The hard part now is organizing and narrowing down to turn this into information you can USE to prioritize your schedule and manage your time better.

So, go over your notes and try and organize all the SPECIFIC discoveries you've made into broader categories like "Adventure," "Success," "Friends/Family," "Career Goals" or whatever seems to fit.

The categories will be different for everyone, but you're trying to assign some meaningful LABELS to the themes that keep coming up in your Heros, your pilgrimages, the skills you want to develop, and all that other stuff.

For me, I feel like "Adventure," "Creativity," "Challenge," and "Success" come back again and again. In my hobbies, my work, my goals, and my heroes, I see these themes written out over and over -

But everyone will have their OWN themes that are most meaningful to them. The trick is UNCOVERING them.

If you've been following along with this exercise, you will have TONS of little "pointers" and hints and clues, all written down in your notebook.

Pause for a few moments again and look at the big picture.

Think about all the information you've just gathered about YOURSELF.

Then zoom out from the details and notes and identify the top one to five themes and categories and WRITE THEM DOWN.

Or, if you have trouble finding your priorities by looking at your notes, think about like this:

If you were looking at notes about a FICTIONAL character, what would that character's priorities seem to be?

You can actually do a character analysis on YOURSELF as if you were a character in a movie or a book.

If you can sort of define the *character*, you can also define *yourself.*

And if you can clearly define your top five life priorities, you will be ahead of 80% of the world.

Most people NEVER spend the time to think clearly about their mission.

Don't put this exercise off till later because you may never come back to it.

In fact, this may be one of the most valuable half-hours of your life if you take it all the way, as far as you can take it.

When you've got your priorities written down, and no more than your top FIVE, I want you to go to the Facebook page (www.Facebook.com/LovetheSAT) and share them!

Now, we've covered a lot in this chapter and I think it's one of the most-important in this whole book.

The main theme has been to spend some time purposefully thinking about your priorities in life so that you can simplify your life and streamline the amount of things you have to focus on.

We've gone through a variety of specific exercises that I have used, and that you can use, to discover your passions and inspirations which will give you renewed energy and improve the quality of your work.

Once you have your list (or even just your one single passion), don't forget to leave a post on the Facebook page (www.Facebook.com/LovetheSAT) because I REALLY want to know what sort of stuff my students are passionate about and I've already shared with you the top five things that I love.

Take your time today to identify your top priorities in life and don't be in any rush to move on through the book. I'll be ready to start again with the next chapter whenever you are!

5. TRACKING YOUR DAYS AND JOURNALING

In this chapter I want to talk about "Productivity Journaling" and how YOU can use it the same way I do:

To track my energy levels, increase my focus on what matters to me, STOP doing things I dislike doing, and track my results towards my most important goals.

Journaling is one of my ABSOLUTE favorite things in life and what I mean is NOT that I love to JOURNAL, because writing actually kind of hurts my wrist after a while...

What I mean is I love the INSIGHTS that come to me when I'm keeping a journal regularly.

I also love that I get more CLARITY about what I LIKE and DISLIKE throughout the day and the week.

Keeping a journal has helped me overcome my blocks at various points in my life and figure out what's causing me any frustration or anxiety that I'm currently feeling.

For example, several years ago simple daily journaling and reflecting helped me realize that I was nearly working myself to death every day trying to grow my business and not taking care of mySELF.

Because of that insight I was able to gradually institute changes that have greatly increased the quality of my life since then -

All because of an easy, little daily journaling habit that EVENTUALLY helped me realize what was right in front of my face: I was working too hard, and it was making me unhappy.

For YOU, I think daily journaling is going to be good for finding your priorities and your times of peak energy.

By tracking what you daydream about - what you WANT to do during the day - you can do what I did and gradually prioritize your time to better focus on stuff that really makes you happy.

Or, if you already KNOW your priorities, journaling is great for researching your own ENERGY LEVELS - on a daily and weekly and even a yearly basis.

For example, I keep several varieties of journals that help me direct my daily energy.

Over the years I've become more of a morning person, but I for long time I still THOUGHT of myself as a late-night person - and it took months of journaling to gradually realize that, actually, I had CHANGED -

What I REALLY looked forward to now was getting up early to make coffee, breakfast, and start to work on my business and music projects.

So that's one MORE thing I learned through a simple journaling habit that boosted my quality of life once I had the insight.

Here's another one: years ago I learned, again through personal journaling, that I am simply UNABLE to work 7 days a week over and over again without a break.

Some of my entrepreneur heroes may be able to do it, but I don't think I can.

So, I scheduled in a MANDATORY "off day" for myself on Fridays and EVENTUALLY I even learned to keep to it.

I am able to make the other 6 days of my week more productive because I make sure to rhythmically include some mandatory breaktime for myself - I can do anything except work on Fridays.

On the yearly basis, I kept a second, VERY simple journal that only had enough room for about half a sentence or about two bullet points per day.

After filling these up for two years, I realized that I had a lot of low points during the Winter but that generally around New Years' I would start to really happy and excited again.

Eventually I could put 2 and 2 together and realized that at the start of winter, business was slow and it was stressful knowing what to do.

But after New Years', my business gets very busy, which takes some of my worries off my mind and puts me in a better mood.

That also indirectly reveals how important my business is to me - if it's doing well, I feel happier, and vice versa.

So journaling, in the second case, can be great for finding your high and low points and learning important lessons for yourself over time in that regard.

Now, journaling has TONS of further uses, but I'm gonna cover a third one right now.

Journaling is great for RECORDING and CELEBRATING progress.

Many people report that once they start tracking their daily results (in fitness, business, school, or whatever), they start to actually GET BETTER RESULTS because now they're paying so much more ATTENTION to whatever it is they are measuring on a daily basis and that ATTENTION helps them IMPROVE faster.

It can be homework assignments completed per day, college apps completed, or whatever. Whatever you're tracking in your journal will DEFINITELY improve over time.

So journaling can be used at the BEGINNING and the END of the day to track three main things:

Number One: Your priorities. Your likes and your dislikes. What was fun and what was miserable during the day.

Number Two: Your energy levels: When do you feel and perform the strongest during each day, week, and year?

Number Three: Your results: What did you accomplish today? What results do you choose to measure?

Intimidated? Don't be. Start small - this is a good exercise even for people who don't like to write, and keep in mind that NOBODY but you will ever see what you write.

Still feel resistant to trying it?

Well, if you really want to improve, you need to try some new habits - that's why you picked up this book! I'm going to STRONGLY encourage you to try all my recommendations out if you want to see real improvement.

Daily journaling at whatever level you can commit to is ALWAYS a good thing - so many great leaders, writers, businesspeople, astronauts, artists, motorcycle racers, or you name it - have kept a journal of some kind.

I PROMISE you won't regret trying this journaling habit out for 30 days, seeing how it helps your figure out our priorities and energy levels, and you can always drop it if you don't like it by then.

Do you keep a journal? And, has it ever helped you learn something useful about yourself?

Before you go on to the next chapter, head over to the Facebook page (www.Facebook.com/LovetheSAT) and tell the rest of us if you've ever tried it before, and what happened!

6. CREATING RHYTHM IN YOUR LIFE (PART 1)

Maybe it's because I studied as a musician, but I like to think about the idea of "RHYTHMS" when it comes to time management.

We will revisit these ideas in the future and use them as a framework for a discussion of high school so get out your pen and paper and be sure to take some notes!

The primary rhythms I observe are hourly, daily, weekly, monthly, and yearly.

Your life is made up of these cycles, so master the rhythms and you could even say that you'll master LIFE!

First, let's look at the hourly rhythm level.

Did you know that MOST humans, even the most brilliant and focused, have a very hard time staying on a challenging task for more than 90 minutes at a time?

It's true - it is REALLY hard, and usually counterproductive, to try and do the same thing for more than an hour and a half straight.

What do you do about this? It's simple.

A stretch or snack break for 5 to 15 minutes each hour or so is generally all you need in most cases and you can sit back down and get back to work.

The idea is to TOTALLY FORGET what you were just working on and do something COMPLETELY DIFFERENT like going for a walk or playing with your family dog.

Something that makes you happy.

If you're truly bored of your main project, you can allow yourself to change activities after the break...

But before you reach that point of giving up, try setting a clock and VOWING to work for 75 to 90 minutes without changing your focus.

Like I said, 90 minutes tends to be the longest that most humans can actually stay highly focused on a single task.

Don't beat yourself up for NOT being able to exceed that limit.

At the end of the 90 minute session you're allowed to completely relax and forget what you were doing.

Trust me, when it comes time to sit down to keep working, it won't be hard to remember where you were.

The thing is, a lot of us feel GUILTY if we take a break when we *think* we're supposed to be working -

Almost like somebody is watching us and judging us for taking a break.

At any age, bosses, parents, peers, and teachers can make us feel guilty for relaxing.

Heck, we can often make OURSELVES feel guilty for relaxing when we're stressed about a project we need to finish.

But, I'm giving you PERMISSION to take a break, and in fact I'm ASKING you to take a break, after a good 90-minute stretch of work and do something that makes you happy.

The key is to do the work FIRST before allowing yourself the reward of the break.

In fact, rewarding yourself regularly is one of the classic tricks of time management!

Coffee works for me - when I finish my 90-minute work session and the timer goes off, I love to pour myself a fresh cup of coffee and take a very physical a stretch break or a quick walk outside.

I also have a few other tricks up my sleeve like quick exercise routines, listening to music and my favorite, playing with the little stray cat that lives outside my house :)

The key is, I've developed my own ideal work rhythm over time, by treating it almost like a personal science project and researching what works, and what doesn't work, by keeping a productivity journal on myself each day.

But, you need to find what works for you!

It's another area where daily journaling can help you discover what helps you quickly relax and regain your energy when you take breaks from work on the hourly or 90-minute level.

Then, when we move up to the DAILY level, it's mainly a question of how we string together our hours.

How do YOU structure your daily rhythm?

Do you plan out your day with a to-do list so as the sun arcs overhead, you can compare your progress through the day to something measurable?

Or, do you simply ensure that you're not wasting time and strive to fill each hour of your day with purpose, fighting towards your primary personal goals in life?

OR... do you not really plan your days, AND not really have a primary goal in life to work towards?

The first two cases are fine - you can either make a to-do list each day...

Even if you DON'T know your "true north" or your main goal in life, you can use your planning skills to continually make each day of your life better than the last day.

That's the power of organization and planning.

OR you can just know EXACTLY what you want to do with your life...

Because then you hardly even NEED a to-do list because most of the time, with a single goal fixed in your mind, you'll just KNOW if what you're doing at the moment is useful towards that goal or not.

That's the power of clarity.

BUT, in the THIRD case, if you DON'T know your primary goal yet, AND you DON'T plan your days at all with an organized to-do list, then you're really just ADRIFT because you don't know where you want to go OR how to get there.

That's why If I had to pick the "most important" rhythm for effective time management, I think I would pick the daily rhythm.

After all, what are weeks, months, and years but big piles of days?

And, you can always lose or waste an hour here or there and things will turn out fine - but waste a whole DAY and you will often find that your WEEK is now wayyyy behind schedule and over-stressed.

I mean, tell me I'm wrong?! If you've ever wasted a whole DAY by accident, or slept so late that you didn't get anything done all day at all, you KNOW it tends to mess up your whole week because you're behind schedule.

And if you have a stressed-out WEEK, that means a whopping 25% of your whole MONTH was stressed out.

So you really can't let the days get away from you because that will reverberate and cause pain in your schedule for quite a while.

Now at the same time, I'll say that a PLANNED, INTENTIONAL day off per week is VERY important for your mental health and sanity -

But the difference is your day off is PLANNED, but a wasted day is NOT planned - it just comes out of nowhere and messes up your whole week.

So again, you can either plan your 24-hour days with an organized to-do list, or you can know your exact number-one life purpose, which allows you to improvise around that and still be highly effective...

But if you don't do EITHER of these things you will probably be generating a great deal of stress and procrastination for yourself in your days and weeks.

If I'm wrong about anything so far, TELL me in the book discussion section!

But after seeing hundreds of high school students go through it, I don't think I'm wrong about this.

Now, your WEEKLY productivity rhythm is MOSTLY just based upon your daily rhythm.

Again, I think the DAILY is the foundational rhythm of all the bigger cycles.

However, you can use your weekly calendar to organize important tasks and chores that you don't want to do every DAY but which must be kept up with regularly - anything from laundry to exercise.

So WEEKS in my mind are more about reminders, chores, and cutting down your stress with a SYSTEM to maintain your life, health, and cleanliness.

Use a weekly schedule to avoid having to re-invent your life constantly.

Actually pause for a moment now, go ahead and brainstorm everything you have to do each week, and pick days for recurring tasks - like "Wednesday and Sunday are gym days" and "Mon-Thursday-Saturday are my vocab days".

Now make sure to WRITE DOWN your weekly plan and put it somewhere you see regularly.

Then keep expanding the concept of rhythm into bigger and bigger time spans - let's think now about your MONTHS.

On a monthly basis, what "chores" or "housekeeping" do you need to do every thirty days or so?

For example, I like to backup my data for my most important projects at least once per month.

That way, even if the unthinkable happens, and my house burns down or something, I'll never lose more than three to four weeks of work (which is still a LOT, but much better than risking the loss of a YEAR or a LIFETIME's worth of work!!)

I also think the monthly level is perfect, for ME at least, to do deep-cleaning of my house, kitchen, bedroom, and workspace.

It's not my FAVORITE thing to do so I can't make myself do it every week, but WHEW when I'm done cleaning, the result is that I'm happier, more organized, I have more SPACE to live and work, and I feel more productive and peaceful.

Monthly rhythms can also be a good level for social obligations and time commitments - for example, have you spent time with your best friends this month? Have you called your grandparents?

What about maintenance needs - anything from your car to your school backpack.

Keep your possessions in good repair so that they don't fail you at a crucial moment when you need them later.

All of this relates to the BIG picture of managing your time and routines to avoid friction and wasted time.

The sky's the limit for monthly routines.

I like to think of monthly routines that enhance my DAILY routines, rather than the other way around.

For example, I deep-clean once a month SO THAT I can do better work each day.

It's NOT that I work every day in order to be able to deep-clean once a month!

And I back up my data each month SO THAT I don't worry about it all day.

It's NOT that I work all day just so I can back up my data at the end of the month!

See what I mean? I think our MONTHLY routines should mostly focus on stuff that empowers your DAILY routine.

After all there are only *12* months per year, but *365* days.

So personally I think the daily routine has the highest impact.

But oftentimes, good DAILY time management is simple - it's just about NOT losing or wasting time for your 16 waking hours.

In contrast, the MONTHLY level demands even FAR more planning and organization on your written calendar since it's easier to loose track of your long-term progress and obligations over 30 days.

Use monthly calendars, backups, and deep-cleaning routines to keep your schoolwork, your workspace, your life, and your mind uncluttered - to reduce waste and improve efficiency.

Monthly rhythms can also include what I call "BIG" weekends, like making sure you do something REALLY fun and cool once a month to rejuvenate yourself and remind yourself why you're working so hard.

For me, the best "BIG" weekends are when I try to go on an all-day motorcycle ride at least once per month -

Just to get out there and find some great roads and forget about emails, work, and cell phones for a whole day.

In fact my rule is that I can NOT check my cell phone or email while I'm out on a motorcycle day.

It's too big of a thing to do EVERY weekend, cause I've gotta plan and get packed and make sure everything is OK back home, plus it takes away a whole productive work day -

But getting out for a big ride once a MONTH is a perfect rhythm for me.

Monthly rhythms can often be some of the EASIEST things to forget about or push to a later date because very rarely do they seem like "urgent priorities."

So, I suggest you pause the video right now and take time to brainstorm up to TEN things that you want to include in your routine every MONTH.

Make sure to include a mix of productivity towards your main goals and your supporting goals, as well as a few points for cleaning, organization, backing up your data, and having some fun each month too.

Finally we have the YEARLY level.

This is my personal FAVORITE because this is where your LIFE goals come in again from the daily level.

See the thing is, you can only do SO MUCH in a single day. But the REAL big progress comes on the YEARLY level.

For example, I remember spending a year writing free educational articles for my website in order to build traffic and attention from potential customers.

I struggled so much at first with the daily effort of writing the articles, until a year passed and I saw the progress our site had made compared to our beginnings - an incredible 500% or FIVE-TIMES increase in website traffic and customers.

Once I saw that, I got super-inspired for the NEXT year's traffic growth.

And then the daily work of writing got a little easier, because instead of thinking about how tired I'd be after three hundred and sixty-five days of blog writing, I was thinking instead about the ONE exciting year of progress we just had and how cool next year was going to be if we kept it up.

So what's the focus of YOUR year, this year?

Knowing this will give you clarity when you need it during the day.

Take a moment to pause and think about your number-one goal for the next twelve months.

Pause your reading to think; write down your answer, and then SHARE it with me on the Facebook page (www.Facebook.com/LovetheSAT).

I think the ideal situation is to have, if possible, JUST ONE yearly goal. This way it's VERY easy to measure your progress towards that one goal.

It's cliché, but I love to use New Year's Eve to set my goalposts for the coming year!

That's what I mean by yearly time-management rhythms.

To review, we all should strive to manage our time on a yearly, monthly, weekly, daily, and hourly level.

The key to establishing a rhythm that works for you is to follow KNOW the number-one thing you want in life, and the number-one thing you want from your year.

In general, your DAILY rhythm is your most important rhythm, so plan and use your days wisely.

In the end, our life and legacy is simply determined by what we choose to do each day.

By understanding how the five rhythms are similar, yet different; connected, yet separate - we can begin to grasp how each level can best be used to manage our own time and to support our primary desires in life.

Now pause for just a moment and share your number-one goal for the next 12 months on the Facebook page (www.Facebook.com/LovetheSAT).

See you again in the next chapter!

7. PLANNERS AND MULTI-CALENDAR TRICKS (PART 1)

In this chapter we're going to go over some of my ideas for physical calendars and planners that you CAN and SHOULD be using to enhance your personal rhythms and direct them towards your primary purpose or purposes in life.

These tips will work very well for high schoolers or anyone who wants to better organize their time and productivity.

We WILL go into more detail on this later on in the next section, particularly when we're discussing how high schoolers can use these planners and the special stuff they should watch out for.

But for now, I just wanted to describe some of my favorite calendar systems and how you might use them.

Let's start with the inexpensive but GIANT dry-erase wall calendar I have up on the wall of my office, which is one of my favorite possessions.

I'm not kidding - this thing is HUGE, like 4 feet by 3 feet.

It's for a whole year so even though it's a giant calendar, each day only has a very small square.

I use this as a mini-journal at the end of each day to record the most essential highlights of the day and a numerical rating from 1 to 10 based on how much I enjoyed my day.

Over time the combo of journaling the highlights plus assigning a rating to the day has led me to some HUGE insights in productivity and personal happiness, so would I highly recommend it to everyone.

Going from hard-copy calendars to digital one, Google Calendar is a fantastic FREE online calendar with automatic reminders, color-coding, event-sharing and more features than I could possibly name.

You can also connect your calendar between all your devices so that updates from your cell phone immediately display on your laptop as well.

Since Google is currently one of the most powerful and productive companies on earth, I believe they probably have one of the best online calendar programs as well.

Of book, insert your favorite online calendar software if you have a different preference. Do some research to find which is right for you!

Online Calendars are an insanely powerful way to keep organized, so if you haven't started using one yet to structure your days, weeks, months, and years, you're behind the curve.

They also function as a searchable database of your past events, which is another way to get some extra utility out of your online calendar.

Now, to take it a little more old-school, actually one of the coolest things you can do for yourself is to get a few awesome monthly wall calendars with cool pictures on a theme that you really like.

For example for me, it's a little silly but pictures of sailboats in beautiful spots, and pictures of super-cool motorcycles really get me psyched up every time I see them, so every year I look forward to ordering the updated calendars with full-color glossy pictures.

It's just one of those things that you can use to get yourself excited about your daydreams and long-term goals, since sometimes during the day you need a little extra inspiration to stay focused and remind you to manage your time well - to remind you of the *rewards* of doing so.

What do you like to daydream about? What gets you super-excited?

Try ordering a couple wall calendars with those themes.

For example, if you go to Amazon.com or your favorite shopping website and and mark "only 5 star reviews" while searching for "Kitten Wall Calendars," I PROMISE you that you will rapidly find some awesome kitten calendars.

Put those calendars somewhere you will see them, and then tell me if it doesn't a little happier and more productive right away!

As you might be able to tell, we've been breaking things down in this chapter from the biggest yearly level, through the monthly level and now to the daily level.

On the daily time-management level, something nice you can do for yourself is get a cool weekly planner.

By "cool" I mean some sort of durable, inspiring planner that will last you a YEAR or more and has some sense of daily and weekly organization built into it.

Pick one that you think is cool-looking and well designed so you will constantly want to open it, write in it, read it and keep track of it.

By the way if you're looking for an incredible selection of daily planners and journals, I will recommend Amazon.com again, as I do for so many other things!

Now for many productive people, the daily to-do list is the most classic and popular way of handling basic time management on a day-to-day basis.

You can even make multiple lists per day - you can make one at breakfast and a revised one at lunch, for example.

Daily to-do lists are definitely a staple of my personal time-management methods.

Along with a giant yearly wall calendar providing me with the BIG perspective, the daily to-do lists keep me chugging along at a slow-and-steady pace.

I use 3 by 5 inch index cards which I constantly crumple up and throw out as I finish them.

3 by 5 inches isn't enough space to fit a ton of to-do items, so it forces me to remain focus on what I need to do first.

The more often I make these type of to-do lists, the more refined my system becomes and now my to-do lists are actually an INCREDIBLY important secret weapon of my productivity.

Also, for the most important daily tasks that you CANNOT afford to forget, use your phone alarm to schedule a reminder!

Finally, for anything from your daily list that doesn't get done but can't be ignored, you can use your ongoing task checklist.

This is basically an "indefinite" list with no limit to how many tasks you can put on it to do in the future.

There's just. one. rule. Anything on this long-term list must have what I call the property of "cross-offability" or in other words, you can ONLY put things on this list if they can ACTUALLY be completed within a reasonable time span - as in, under two hours.

If it would take more than two hours, find a way to break it down into sub tasks and THOSE are what should go on your to-do list because THOSE are smaller sub-tasks that you can accomplish in a reasonable time.

For example, "Win Scholarship Money" can NOT go on this to-do list because it's too open-ended and has NO finish point; it does NOT obey "Cross-offability".

Instead, you must break the task down into smaller bullets, for example:

1) Create a list of five potential scholarships to apply for.
2) Draft your re-usable scholarship resume.
3) Complete each of the five applications one-by-one.
4) Go the post office to send them in.
5) Find five more scholarships and repeat the process until college is paid for.

If any of THOSE steps still look daunting, break it down into sub-sub-steps until you're faced with a simple task that can be completed in under a couple of hours.

If you don't follow this rule the ongoing-task list will just spiral out of control with tasks that can't actually be completed and removed from the list and cause you anxiety since we can always THINK of waaaaay more ideas than we can actually do.

Try to keep it focused and only add tasks to this ongoing list if they are important AND they contribute towards your top passions AND that they are tasks which can actually be completed and aren't just open-ended goals or dreams.

So to review this chapter, we've covered some timeless methods we can use to track and organize our time -

From the giant yearly dry-erase calendar, to monthly wall calendars with inspiring photographs, down through weekly and daily planners and to-do lists.

Remember, the purpose of all this documentation and calendar-use is to HELP you, not to slow you down!

You don't have to use EVERYTHING I've just listed - just pick the one or two methods that you think will help you overcome your scheduling weak spots, and try to make them part of your daily habits.

So now I've told you ALL about my own personal system for using multiple types of calendars to solve a bunch of scheduling problems that I used to have.

Now turn to yourself:

What sort of calendars do YOU like to use, and how do you use them?

And, what sort of fun PICTURES do you like to get on YOUR monthly wall calendars?

Let us know how YOU'RE using your calendars, and how well your methods are working for you, on the Facebook page (www.Facebook.com/LovetheSAT) right now, and I'll see you in the next chapter!

8. HEALTH, FITNESS, SLEEP, AND TIME MANAGEMENT

This next chapter is all about improving time management through your HEALTH, as seen through the lens of the sleep and the physical activity that you are getting on a daily and weekly basis.

We're not going to go into this like a medical doctor because I'm not one - but sleep and fitness are SUPER important to your overall ability to manage your time!

The problem is for about 99% of us these days, sleep and fitness START getting pushed back in high school, and it just gets worse through college, and then into the working world, and you never really have the time to change your habits and get healthy.

So it doesn't SEEM urgent but it is.

It is really really URGENT to make sure that you have good sleep and fitness habits because in the blink of an eye you will be 10 or 20 years older and you will FEEL good or bad based on how you've been treating your body during that time.

Sleep and fitness EMPOWER everything else we are talking about in this book, like having the clarity to set your goals, the energy to pursue them and the tenacity to overcome the obstacles along the way.

If you are healthy and rested, managing your time will become significantly easier -

Or to put that another way, if you're tired and sick, it's virtually impossible to use your days to maximum effectiveness, right?

Now when it comes to sleep...

I'm no sleep expert, but common wisdom and my own experience suggest that seven to ten hours of sleep every twenty-four hours is about right for keeping your health strong and your energy levels high.

Now notice I said "every twenty-four hours" not "every night."

A mid-day NAP is a GREAT backup option for sleep, particularly if you were unable to get a full night's sleep for any reason.

If you have an off-period in the middle of the school day, sometimes the best use of it simply to get a 45-minute power nap in a quiet corner.

Likewise, sometimes the best use of a weekend is simply to catch up on a bunch of sleep after a particularly insane week.

Now it's not always easy to find time for a midday nap -

So the key is to PLAN AHEAD whenever possible and try to make a habit of finishing your work EARLY.

That reduces emergency situations that are going to eat into your sleep AND prevent you from catching up with naps when you need it.

Basically, as always, getting BEHIND just tends to snowball and get worse if you start to slide.

There's a lot more we could say about sleep -

For example, we could discuss the ENORMOUS impact that all the constantly-glowing TV and computer screens, video games and social media have on our sleep health..

But for now let's just agree that getting good sleep is incredibly important and not optional.

If you have to get up EARLY for school, there's only one option and that's to go to BED early - because if you go to bed LATE and you have to wake up EARLY you WILL be tired.

It's just MATH - nothing personal.

So you have to avoid that situation if at all possible; the lack of sleep will ripple outwards and probably you'll struggle to get back on track for a few days afterwards.

Now, one really cool thing about my next suggestion, which is EXERCISE, is that it also helps with my first suggestion about sleep -

Because when you EXERCISE during the day your body is more ready for SLEEP at the end of the day!

Now don't misunderstand me - I'm not saying that exercise will STEAL your energy and make you pass out at the end of the day.

In fact, quite the opposite - daily exercise GIVES you energy, rather than taking it away.

But hard exercise ALSO helps you get a good night's sleep at the end of the day.

Again, this isn't the time to talk in detail because I'm not a doctor or health professional, but I just had to point out the importance of physical activity and remind you that it needs to form part of your time-management plan.

Not only do you need to schedule in some physical activity on a regular basis, it's also going to pay itself back in the form of additional energy and clarity to pursue your goals.

There is an INFINITE variety of fun and cool ways to stay healthy and I promise there's at least one thats fit YOU perfectly if you go and look for it.

Humans have been making up games, sports, exercises, and stretches probably since the dawn of time, so you have TONS of choice in what to participate in.

Decide on your health goals and then do your research.

For example, do you want a stronger heart and lungs? Check out cardio exercise for endurance.

Maybe you want to bulk up and get stronger - go for strength training and muscle-building.

Perhaps you don't really care about exercise unless there's COMPETITION: you should be on a soccer, football, or volleyball team!

There are so many options: individual and team sports; competitive or friendly teams; or even competing against yourself.

For example, have you thought about rock climbing as a form of exercise? Hiking and camping? Dance? Cheerleading?

Don't lock yourself into pre-established molds of assuming you hate sports and exercise just because you've had a few bad experiences in the past.

For me, sport motorcycling, archery, bicyling, long walks through nature, and low-key jogging are my favorite ways to get exercise.

I also throw in some simple bodyweight exercises I can do at home which basically means stuff with a minimum of equipment like pushups, pullups, and walking or jogging.

I do this because it makes me feel good and it's a nice stretch in between typing on the computer, answering phones and emails, and work stuff like that.

Now, speaking of finding activities that FIT you, I'm not the biggest guy on the field, so although I'm competitive at heart I can't really crush it in basketball or football or whatever so the so-called "standard" team sports -

That's probably not where I'm going to enjoy myself the most.

That's not actually a big deal because at the same time I don't LOVE to run around and sweat a ton, I prefer to eat right, get some daily moderate exercise in ways I enjoy, and I'm not trying to be the next big movie or sports star with my physique.

See? Since I know what my REAL life goals are, I'm comfortable accepting a decent level of fitness.

Even though I'd LIKE to be a super-human, the level I'm currently at SUPPORTS my life goals without taking too much time and attention away from them.

By the way, need help finding time for all this sleep and exercise stuff?

That's just one reason you need priorities set straight.

SOMETHING may have to get dropped from your schedule, but it CANNOT be your health.

NO human can afford to ignore sleep and fitness. To do so is ultimately counterproductive.

Being sick is just a HUGE waste of time.

Make sure to get the nightly sleep and daily physical activity it takes to perform at your peak.

The time you invest into your health will pay itself back with longer life and increased energy, and you'll have fun along the way when you spend time on activities you enjoy.

What are YOU doing to keep yourself healthy and well-rested?

Take a moment to pause and share your health and fitness routines on the Facebook page (www.Facebook.com/LovetheSAT) and I'll see you in the next chapter!

9. GREAT QUOTES ON TIME MANAGEMENT

In this chapter, I wanted to step back from my own methods for time management, goal-setting and productivity and focus instead on what other people have said about it.

I feel like I've learned a lot about life by overhearing great quotes from super-smart people and I wanted to share some that I've found on the subject of time management and offer a little commentary about why I liked each quote.

As we go along, please be sure to PAUSE and COPY DOWN any quotations you particularly like and put them somewhere you will see them on a regular basis!

The first set of quotes deals with the subject of FOCUS:

I like these because they agree with my belief that, if possible, we should each choose our top, number-one focus in life in order to reach our highest potential.

Tony Robbins - author, entrepreneur, and speaker - said:

> *"One reason so few of us achieve what we truly want is that we never direct our focus; we never concentrate our power.*
>
> *"Most people dabble their way through life, never deciding to master anything in particular."*

From this quote we learn that we should identify our top one to five priorities as soon as possible and concentrate our powers upon them.

Alexander Graham Bell (inventor of the telephone) said:

> *"Concentrate all your thoughts upon the work at hand. The sun's rays do not burn until brought to a focus."*

This quote, from the inventor of the TELEPHONE, which billions of people use every day, is perfect proof that we should make the wise choice of focusing our attention on a LIMITED number of goals.

Zig Ziglar (an author, speaker, and legendary salesman) said:

> *"Lack of direction, not lack of time, is the problem. We all have twenty-four hour days."*

Zig Ziglar had a funny name, but he was a fantastic businessman.

This quote is a great reminder that we all have the same amount of time in the day.

Some of us just put it to better use than others by SETTING THEIR DIRECTION and sticking to it with focus.

The next few quotes deal with the topics of planning, action, and execution.

I like *these* quotes because I think I'm at my best when I'm ACTING on my dreams.

It can be hard to get started and to maintain action, so learn from the best in the following quotes:

Dwight Eisenhower, U.S. President and Commanding General during World War II, said:

> *"In preparing for battle I have always found that plans are useless, but planning is indispensable."*

This quotation comes from a battle-tested commanding general in one of the biggest armed conflicts of human history -

And *he's* telling us to PLAN ahead of time so that we can IMPROVISE when reality actually hits and things start to get a little nuts.

When you feel like life is a battlefield and you're overwhelmed with demands on your attention, it's especially important to make your time for your battle plan!

Although plans ALWAYS change, you'll be more prepared because you made your plan A, plan B and plan C long *before* the battle started.

Abraham Lincoln, one of the greatest U.S. Presidents, said:

> *"Give me six hours to chop down a tree and I will spend the first four sharpening the axe."*

This whimsical and simple quote, whether it was truly said by Abe Lincoln or not, reminds us that wise preparations are two-thirds of good time management.

Now, don't misinterpret this to mean that you should spend a lot of time planning instead of chopping.

Keep in mind, Abe wasn't *sitting around* for four hours before going to work!

In fact, his whole plan was really only two steps long: Step 1) sharpen axe, step 2) chop tree.

Abe wasn't *planning* for those four hours, he was *preparing*. There's a tremendous difference but we often mix the two up.

He spend four hours of hard work sharpening, followed by another two good hours of cutting.

The important thing is that, once he knew his specific goal of chopping the tree, he wisely budgeted his time with a simple plan from the beginning to the end - leading to the fastest and most efficient outcome.

Napoleon Hill, productivity researcher and grandfather of the self-improvement genre, told us:

> *"Create a definite plan for carrying out your desire and begin at once, whether you are ready or not, to put this plan into action."*

Napoleon Hill is a favorite author of mine and he knew EVERYTHING there is to know about becoming successful, productive and happy because he spend twenty years personally interviewing hundreds of the smartest and most successful people alive in his day, in every possible industry and field.

Then he wrote about the common threads that united successful people, and one of them was taking action BEFORE everything was "perfect."

He's considered the "grandfather" of the self-improvement industry and continues to be read around the world by people like you and me who want to get more out of life.

Another way of saying Mr. Hill's idea is "don't wait for all the lights to turn green before leave your home to start driving."

Make the best plan you can, then begin IMMEDIATELY to put it into action.

If you can do this, you'll pretty much already be in the top 20% of the competition.

On the subject of energy and personal efficiency, Tony Robbins said:

> *"The higher your energy level, the more efficient your body.*
>
> *The more efficient your body, the better you feel and the more you will use your talent to produce outstanding results."*

This quote from productivity guru Tony Robbins reminds us how incredibly important our physical health and vitality are.

Whenever possible, we should be keeping ourselves healthy, well-fed, and well-exercised.

Keeping our bodies in good health makes it easier for us to get results in our school, creative work, and career!

On the subjects of procrastination and wasting time, the following two quotes apply:

Bruce Lee, actor, martial artist, and cultural icon, said:

> *"If you spend too much time thinking about a thing, you'll never get it done."*

Bruce Lee was a master of discipline and action, so take his advice - don't THINK too much - just DO!

Be like a karate master - you're either training, fighting, or meditating.

Everything is focused on your ultimate goal, and you never waste time hesitating or sitting around and thinking too much.

Thomas Sowell, noted economist and author, opined that:

> *"The least productive people are usually the ones who are most in favor of holding meetings."*

Use this quote as a reminder to NOT be the person calling another group meeting.

Instead, be the one who GETS THINGS DONE and barely has TIME for attending meetings.

And, to may to go a little counter to everything all the other advice so far, here's one last bit of wisdom about using your time to the fullest:

Author Marthe Troly-Curtin gave us this classic quote about taking it easy from time to time:

> *"Time you enjoy wasting is not wasted time."*

Of course, this one reminds us that as long as we're enjoying ourselves and having a good time in life then we are "doing it right" -

So never feel guilty about having a good time doing stuff you love with people you care about!

That's a short list of my favorite quotes from interesting and famous people talking about time management and productivity.

I've discovered that their words can be an incredibly-useful inspiration that I can use to boost my OWN energy!

Their words give me energy and remind me that I'm not the first person to struggle with time management.

Remember to pick at least one of the quotes, copy it down, and put it somewhere you will see it!

Do YOU have a favorite quote about time management - either from my list, one you already know, or a quote you recently found?

Please pause to SHARE it with us on the Facebook page (www.Facebook.com/LovetheSAT) so we can all be inspired by it and then I'll meet you in the next chapter!

10. THE BEST BOOKS ON TIME MANAGEMENT (PART 1)

There's an old saying: "if you read the best three books on a topic, you'll be in the top ten percent of experts in the world on that subject."

It's totally true - most people don't realize how EASY it is to self-educate yourself on ANY topic under the sun just by reading a few key books, and time management is no different.

So let's go two better and get FIVE of the best books on time management and productivity for ANY age.

Here's a quick list of the five books:

1. Getting Things Done by David Allen.
2. 15 Secrets Successful People Know About Time Management by Kevin Kruse.
3. Eat That Frog! by Brian Tracy.
4. The Seven Habits of Highly Effective People by Stephen Covey.
5. The Power of Habit by Charles Duhigg.

Let me give you a quick overview of each book so you can decide if it's something you'd like to investigate further and order for your personal library.

I'd highly recommend any of them so pick one or more that SOUND good to you and catch your attention - choose by INSTINCT and pick the ones that sounds the best to YOU.

Here we go!

Getting Things Done: The Art of Stress-Free Productivity by David Allen is considered "the bible" of personal productivity.

Written by one of the most in-demand business coaches in the world, I believe it's the single all-time best-selling book on personal and business productivity.

Mr. Allen likes to mix the PRACTICAL and the THEORETICAL, the INTELLECTUAL and the EMOTIONAL in his approach to time management - just like I do!

So, not only will this book help with specific techniques but also broader principles.

This book is definitely aimed more towards businesspeople and adults, but it's a great read for a mature high schooler.

The next book is **15 Secrets Successful People Know About Time Management** by Kevin Kruse.

This is an AWESOME, research-based book that uses real-life heros of productivity as the basis for examples you can imitate in your own life.

The subtitle of the book is "The productivity habits of seven billionaires, thirteen olympic athletes, twenty-nine straight-A students and two hundred and thirty nine entrepreneurs."

As the subtitle of this book suggests, the author interviewed billionaires, straight-A students, olympic athletes, and hundreds of entrepreneurs to find what made them so efficient and productive -

Then he connected the dots and provided a formula you can use for your own time management skills.

Definitely pick this one up - I love motivational books based on REAL people and REAL interviews.

Eat That Frog! 21 Great Ways to Stop Procrastinating and Get More Done in Less Time by Brian Tracy is another classic by a legendary coach and author.

This book focuses on how to STOP PROCRASTINATING so it's like coming at the problem from the opposite angle -

Instead of saying "how do I use time BETTER" it's about how to stop WASTING time.

Based on the psychology of wasted time, this book is great for anyone who finds their days and weeks slipping away from them because they aren't taking action.

Book four, **The Seven Habits of Highly Effective People**, by Stephen R Covey is another popular classic.

The seven habits of this book are common to all hard-working and highly effective professionals and students.

This book has remained a bestseller for 25 years!

Now that's not an accident, it's because millions of people have found it helpful for improving the effectiveness of their own time-management.

Finally, book five is **The Power of Habit: Why We Do What We Do in Life and Business** by Charles Duhigg.

This book spent over a year on the New York Times bestseller list and it is absolutely HUGE in terms of opening your eyes to the power of habits both good and bad.

It's one of the easiest reads on this list and one that can help you tackle perhaps the MOST important element of time management - your DAILY HABITS.

I'm going to give one final bonus mention to Think and Grow Rich by Napoleon Hill.

Published around the time of the American Great Depression, this classic contains inspirational wisdom that the author collected after TWENTY YEARS of interviewing the most successful businesspeople, leaders, and stars of his era.

Even though it might be my PERSONAL favorite, I don't include it in this list of the top five because it's pretty OLD-school and may be a tougher read for some high school students, whereas the five books I've recommended will be much more up-to-date and feel "modern" and easy to read.

However for the true connoisseur, I do *highly* rate "Think and Grow Rich" because it covers comprehensive tips on setting goals and consistently reaching them -

Again, these are LITERALLY the same tips that people like titans of industry and famous Hollywood stars use to reach the top levels of achievement and fame.

So that's a great 6th bonus book that absolutely deserves a mention any time you're talking about time management.

Now, there are TONS of great books on time management that I'm brushing over - but these FIVE (or six) will be a fantastic start to your personal library.

You can order any or all of these books on Amazon.com. Be sure to check out other reader reviews and "look inside" the books before you buy!

Do you have a favorite book about productivity, time management, or following your dreams?

If so, please share the title and author on the Facebook page (www.Facebook.com/LovetheSAT), and let me know which of these books you're ordering.

See you in the next chapter!

QUIZ #2: REVIEW OF TIMELESS TIME MANAGEMENT

Welcome to the second quiz of Ultimate Time Management for Teens and Students!

Remember, it's all about memory and recall.

There's no time limit. Go slowly and try to get them all correct.

Answers are on p.188.

QUESTION #1: What is Timeless Rule #1 of Time Management?

A) Know what you want to DO with your life.
B) Know what your PARENTS want for you in life.
C) Know yourself and your personal rhythms.
D) Do everything you can to get more FREE time.

QUESTION #2: What does "The State of Flow" refer to?

A) When you're getting all your assignments turned in on-time and not falling behind.
B) The strategic time-management approach of "flowing like water" in order to meet all the demands of your busy high school schedule.
C) The process of stacking up extracurriculars to build a strong college-application resume.
D) When you lose track of time ENGAGED in something CHALLENGING that you care about or love to do.

QUESTION #3: Why should you keep a daily journal?

A) To track your productivity.
B) To learn more about your personal energy levels.
C) To celebrate your progress and results.
D) To document and discover what makes you HAPPY and UNHAPPY.
E) To assign quality ratings to your days.
F) All of the above and more!

QUESTION #4: What is the longest period of time that most human beings can stay focused on a single challenging task without taking a break?

A) 15 minutes - long enough for a few YouTube videos.
B) 60 minutes - long enough for most high school classes.
C) 90 minutes - long enough to complete most small and medium-sized tasks.
D) 3 hours - long enough for most college classes.
E) 8 hours - an average adult's work day.
F) Up to 24 hours under intense, life-or-death pressure.

QUESTION #5: What does the Rule of Cross-Offability refer to?

A) Get rid of EVERY class or activity that you don't want to be a part of!
B) Your calendars and to-do lists should only have tasks that can be COMPLETED in a reasonable span (several hours at most).

QUESTION #6: How much sleep does the average human need per night?

A) 7 to 10 hours per night.
B) 10 to 11 hours per night.
C) 5 to 7 hours per night.
D) Sleep is for the weak.

QUESTION #7: Who was Napoleon Hill?

A) Inventor of the telephone.
B) Grandfather of the self-improvement genre, author of "Think and Grow Rich," and interviewer of dozens of famous leaders and successful celebrities.
C) My time-management professor in college.
D) A legendary salesman and businessman who was excellent at managing his time.

QUESTION #8: There's an old saying that goes "If you read the top three books on a subject..."

A) "You'll be able to write a book of your own."
B) "You might as well just become a teacher."
C) "You'll be in the top 10% of experts in that field."
D) "You are just scratching the surface of the topic."

ANSWERS ON p.188.

11. HOW TO USE YOUR TOP 1-5 PRIORITIES TO POWER UP YOUR TIME IN HIGH SCHOOL

Now we're going to be talking about how the GENERAL advice on time management from the last section (Chapters 3-10) **can be directly applied to the specific challenges faced by teenagers HIGH SCHOOL.**

This chapter is all about using self-knowledge to make high school a better and more useful experience for you.

First, go back to the chapter in the previous section on identifying your top one to five priorities in life.

If you didn't already make progress towards identifying your top 1-5 priorities, then head back to that chapter and brainstorm THAT topic until you got at least SOME sort of results written down, PLEASE back up and go do it now, because it's 100% mandatory for *this* (and upcoming) chapters to work.

So, in that chapter we discussed A TON of methods for discovering your passions like:

- Journaling on what you consistently DAYDREAM about when you're bored with something else.

- Asking, what puts you in a state of FLOW that you can't wait to get back in to?

- Making a list of the people, figures, and characters who are your heroes and heroines, and analyzing THEIR character for clues to your own.

- Asking yourself what PILGRIMAGES do you want to make - where to, and why?

- Or, what skills do you like to use, practice, and hone in your day-to-day life?

After all the brainstorming was done, we also talked about identifying main categories that might be called stuff like "adventure" or "success" or "family and friends" or "athletic excellence" or WHATEVER keeps coming up as most important to you.

Now, I want to tell you a couple of stories about two good friends of mine from high school, as well as return to my own story about figuring out what to do with MY life because I think that DIRECTLY relates to your own current situation.

The first story is probably what I would call the "happiest" although it's not the only happy ending.

This is the story of my high school friend, whom I'll call "Sam," who had a HUGE passion for movies.

He knew EVERYTHING about all the actors, the plots, the directors and special effects, for as long as I've known him...

He's always wanted to WRITE and DIRECT movies EVER since high school.

ALL his passion and focus was directed around it since the day we met.

In high school he organized film groups, got teachers to help him out, and even worked with the local city film groups.

It was a cinch for him to get into NYU for film school, which is known as one of the best places for young directors to study.

He continued to find many friends and people who had similar dreams and they all supported each other in their movie-making dreams.

And, before he was 28, he'd already found investors and directed a full-length feature movie with his friends that premiered at several film festivals.

Now he's planning his next movie and I'm sure he'll take the lessons from the first one and continue to press forward towards his dreams.

It's really inspiring and I think we could all afford to learn something from his example!

Now, in my OWN story, I feel like I've done PRETTY well in terms of finding my passions and working towards life goals that matter to me although not QUITE as impressively well as Sam has done so far!

I've NEVER been able to boil myself down to just ONE passion, and at best I've got it down for three or four -

like I've said, my favorite things are music, motorcycle travel, and building my business - and I feel lucky to have discovered these passions before I was 30

(Not that there's *anything* wrong with figuring it out AFTER 30, either - but it's do think it's nice to KNOW what you want to use your life for as soon as you possibly can!)

If I have any real regret, it's just that I didn't start SOONER on my goals of music and entrepreneurship, because ever since I started TRUSTING myself, things have come together better and better.

For example, back in 7th grade, I was good with electronics and I already had the idea to start a computer company, at a time when that sort of thing was actually highly in-demand...

(Although I didn't even know at the time that that's how an businessperson would describe my idea)

... BUT, the adults around me kind of discouraged me from trying it, because I'd need to borrow money from outside investors or friends or family, and I was a 7th grader so who knows if THAT would have worked.

Anyway, because of THAT sort of negative experience, it was about 15 years before I ever considered the idea of starting a company again -

But turns out, I actually LOVE starting my own businesses and projects and stuff and I'm pretty good at it because it just fits my personality and skills very well.

So even though I feel like my story has a happy ending, I still know I could be WAY ahead of where I am now if ONLY I'd noticed and TRUSTED my passions sooner.

That's one of the things that *really* motivates me to write this book -

I want YOU to find your passions years earlier than I did, because I TRULY believe that the world is a better place if we're all working hard on the things we care most about.

Now, I've got a somewhat more unfortunate story to tell you.

This is the story of a friend, who I'll call James, who followed through on what he thought OTHER people respect and what he thought OTHER people would pay well for.

He started off REALLY strong in high school - working on things he cared about like artistic and creative projects, which he was really good at it.

But, over time he somehow lost his way and every time I met him he seemed MORE and MORE focused on OTHER people's goals that didn't seem like HIM any more.

He's worked REALLY hard, just like I have - but despite the fact that he and I have both worked quite hard, he seems very UNHAPPY, and I think it's because he hasn't gotten closer to what HE truly cares about -

I'm sure he'll get there, because I believe in him in as a friend and a fellow human being, but personally, I think it's just better to avoid this whole situation in the first place.

Try not to follow the path of James's example where you STOP doing what you truly care about - maybe because you're worried it's not respected or well-paid enough or your friends won't think it's cool or your family won't approve....

Because in the end no one else's approval matters more than your own.

If you're seeking someone ELSE's approval as your own measure of success, then no matter HOW hard you work, you will NEVER - EVER - be able to get close enough to the happiness that you seek!

You have to decide for yourself what matters in life. It's as easy and as difficult as that.

Here are the lessons we can take from all this for the purposes of our book.

The happiest people I know have focused on their top priorities from as early as possible.

That means they DON'T measure their success or their path in OTHER people's eyes -

You HAVE to measure it by your progress on the top one to five things that YOU actually care about -

Knowing and understanding this principle might be the MOST IMPORTANT thing you EVER learn in life because it's the ONLY rule that can lead to you being fulfilled, happy, and productive, and those traits absolutely RADIATE out into the rest of your life and eventually improve the lives of everyone else around you.

The more I do what I LOVE, the more it seems to attract and help the people around me because I'm POWERED UP and I have tons of energy and knowledge to share because I CARE so much, because I'm working on my NATURAL PASSIONS that no one had to TELL me to follow!

Get it? You want to work on the stuff that NO ONE has to FORCE you to do - the stuff that you NEVER WANT TO STOP doing!

Like movies, motorcyling, starting businesses, helping people, teaching people, saving lives, seeing the world, helping people get healthy, or telling incredible stories - POWERFUL dreams like these will make YOU powerful too.

You can ONLY properly manage your time in high school IF You know YOUR top priorities and they aren't somebody else's.

You don't have to be PERFECT or EXACTLY RIGHT about your life priorities in high school, although the closer you can get, the better.

What matters MOST right now is that you pause and take time to SERIOUSLY think about what I'm saying, and even work it out with a pen and paper until you reach your next level of insight into yourself -

Ask youself this:

What do you REALLY FREAKIN' CARE ABOUT when no one else is watching?

NOT "what's highly paid," "what does my family want", "what would my friends think is cool."

Are there any goals you're pursuing right now that are NOT your own goals, but somebody else's?

Maybe these impresonal activities, these uses of your youth, your ability to learn, and your precious and limited time on earth, are making you feel a feeling of EXHAUSTION, DREAD, or DISGUST, or BOREDOM, or HATRED.

Can take some time RIGHT NOW to PAUSE and LIST some of these "fake goals" that DON'T get you excited even though they are a LOT of work and mental energy?

In my opinion, success in life is partially about the difficult work of CUTTING OUT fake and impersonal goals from our days so that we have the crucial time for our real dreams in these brief and fast-moving human lives that we're limited to.

This is literally a matter of LIFE and DEATH - so don't put up with fake goals a single day longer.

Put the book down, do a heavy brainstorm, and journal yourself a list of stuff you should CUT OUT of your life because it doesn't truly feel meaningful to you.

Here are a few of my final takeaway thoughts.

The sooner you know what you love, the better.

High school is NOT too early to get it figured out, as my movie-making friend Sam proved to me.

Don't try to please others. It's actually impossible, and it will never make you truly happy.

Your classes in high school do NOT necessarily help you discover what you love in life.

People around you do NOT necessarily help you discover it either, unless YOU already have a compass direction for yourSELF to follow -

Then they can rally around your sense of purpose and help you a great deal even from a young age.

Again, think of my movie-making friend Sam as your example.

The more time you spend "researching yourself," journaling and taking notes on your daydreams, the sooner you will discover what TRULY matters to you.

Finally, if you are serious about something, and you know what you're talking about, you *will* be taken seriously even if you are young - at least by SOME teachers -

And luckily, those will be the RIGHT teachers to help you on the way to your dreams.

Now, if you haven't already taken notes and made SIGNIFICANT progress towards identifying YOUR top one to five goals that I keep going on about, then I want you to STOP and go back through this entire chapter, as well as the entire previous chapter on "Identifying your top 1-5 goals in life"

That's right, if you're not there yet, I want you to REREAD and REDO these two chapters before you go on because this is one of the most serious parts of the whole book and YOU must work it out yourself -

I can't tell you the answer from a pre-written page - I would if I could, but there's just no way.

So please, pause and spend at least 15 or 30 minutes working on this now.

I don't think it's worth rushing past this step just to be the first person to get to the last page of the book.

You need to *discover*, or at least GUESS based on your current personality, your top one to five goals in life and prioritize them as clearly as you possibly can.

There's NO reason to rush on through the book before you've made progress on this assignment.

Don't fall for the trap of believing you're too young or too inexperienced to start to figuring it out today, this very hour.

I PROMISE, the sooner you have your dreams and life goals sorted out, and the sooner you can CONFIDENTLY say "who you are"...

Then the more effectively you can manage your time even starting NOW in high school,

And the happier, more productive, and more successful you will be for the rest of your life, I PROMISE.

So, QUESTION for you before you go handle all that stuff, and please share your answer on the Facebook page! (www.Facebook.com/LovetheSAT)

What is YOUR number-one dream that you can start working towards in high school?

Or, if you're like me and you can't seem to completely narrow it down, what are your top two to five dreams or goals?

Leave us a quick post about it on the Facebook wall to get yourself psyched up about all the great work you're doing, and I'll see you in the next chapter.

12. CREATING RHYTHM IN YOUR LIFE (PART 2)

Welcome to part TWO of my thoughts on the concept of creating *rhythm* in your life...

Which might be something that resonates more with *creative*-minded people than analytical-minded people, but if you're interested just keep reading and hopefully I'll provide some useful thoughts along the way.

I just want to warn you though, this is a really BIG chapter that doesn't have the same IMMEDIATE payoff that most of the other chapters do -

This one is more abstract and raises a lot of themes that I think are really important - but it's not necessarily for everyone.

This chapter is about PERSPECTIVE - as much of it as I can provide, since I'm nearly 29 years old, which isn't THAT old but it's definitely not THAT young -

And not everything in this chapter fits into a clean or simple soundbite or quote - but I still think there's a TON to be learned from the upcoming info.

So, I just wanted to set that expectation so I don't disappoint you - and if you're ENJOYING and GETTING something out of this chapter, please read all the way through and use Facebook (www.Facebook.com/LovetheSAT) to let me know what you think at the end!

Now, if you back up and review your notes to the first chapter on Creating Rhythm in your schedule, you'll recall that we discussed concepts of momentum and energy and cycles of life that operate on small, medium, large and LIFE-long levels...

And, if you become more CONSCIOUS of those cycles operating on multiple HIGH levels, you tend to become MUCH more mature and skilled in the art of time management on the daily and hourly level.

It might sound a little mysterious or "sci-fi" but I promise that these levels and this energy are AROUND you and IN you and they can help you if you learn more about them...

(Which, by the way, is another thing that JOURNALING has helped me with at the end of each day.)

So now, let's think about how the idea of rhythm applies to your time management in high school.

High School is an absurdly busy time of life for ambitious high schoolers.

Between sports, athletics and everything else, it can be easy to burn out.

The truth is, as a general principle, it's much easier to KEEP things rolling than to START things rolling again.

What I mean is, if you can stay in motion you'll find it easier to get everything done that's being thrown at you.

But, if you burn out - even for a couple of days - you can end up being CRUSHED by the pile-up of work - so it's important to keep yourself sane at the same time as you push your hardest.

Now THAT is a balancing act.

So I ask: Are you pushing your energy and productivity to the max each week while NOT burning yourself out from overwork?

Do your time-management rhythms include time to relax and really ENJOY yourself - about 10 to 20 percent of your work time?

Furthermore, in the midst of all the DAILY and WEEKLY rhythms of your busy life, are you planning your YEARLY and LIFETIME rhythms so that you don't just get tossed about by school and the world around you?

This chapter involves all the different tempos and speeds of life and how they fit together to produce our entire experience from the hours in our days, to the years in our lives, and although we won't go THIS deep in today's chapter, this also affects the generations of lives that make up the entire human race.

For now let's keep our ambitious a LITTLE more modest and start with the HOURLY level.

For most of us, HOURLY rhythms tend to be about phases of effort and relaxation, or tension and release.

Sometimes you're working, sometimes you're chilling.

One of my FAVORITE descriptions of this natural human condition was an famous author, whose name I forgot, writing to a friend of his:

He said, "I am constantly torn between my desire to SAVE the world and to SAVOR the world."

Of book, in French it sounds even better!!

What I think he meant by that phrase, how I interpret it is, he was torn by his desire to BUCKLE DOWN and work on his GREAT BOOKS, because he was a famous and great author working on his passion -

He KNEW he could help "SAVE" the world by producing great literature, but sometimes it's so HARD to do that -

It takes so much TIME and ENERGY and FOCUS and WORK and WILLPOWER -

Do you think it's EASY even for a great, famous, and successful novelist to close the doors, shut the blinds and sit at his typewriter for hours until he produces his next great work to save the world?

NO - no matter HOW famous or successful you currently are, it's ALWAYS going to take hard work to save the world -

But it should always MATTER to you and make you feel like you CONTRIBUTE to the world through your work.

It feels, actually, like you're SAVING the world through giving your deepest gifts to the world.

But, at the same time this author was torn.

He wanted to SAVOR the world - to ENJOY the fruits of his labor, maybe go to the cafe and be recognized and honored for his fame for an hour -

Maybe it was a sunny day and he just wanted to sit down in a field for the day and enjoy it WITHOUT thinking about how he could include the scene in his next book.

Likewise, I tend to think racecar drivers have one of the coolest jobs on the planet.

BUT - I REALIZE that sometimes even THEY get SICK of having to drive, practice in the heat, give up time they could be spending with friends or on vacation, or they get tired of having to travel all over the place for races.

See, even in high school, and even in the middle of the COOLEST possible career we could imagine for ourselves, we're torn between SAVING the world and SAVORING the world.

SAVING the world is doing your homework, studying for exams, getting a jump on college preparations.

SAVORING the world is hanging out with your friends, playing computer games, lounging by the pool all day, going on a Sunday drive with your parents and the family dog.

Unfortunately, you can't always SAVE the world at the same time you're SAVORING it - and vice versa.

Picture an action hero stopping to smell the roses at the same time as he fights off evil - doesn't really work, does it?

On the other hand, I have a personal example that proves that exceptions to this rule ARE possible:

When I was studying piano, it DID kind of feel like I was "SAVING" the world, by practicing piano as much as I could, at the same time as I was "SAVORING" it, because of how much I loved playing the piano.

So, I believe in SOME circumstances it's possible to both save and savor at the same time - but only when you're working on your PASSIONS and true personal compass in life.

And EVEN THEN - I would absolutely HAVE to take breaks during the day for food, coffee, going outside, stretching, exercise, and other stuff to change it up from just doing piano all the time.

On an HOURLY basis, we CHOOSE whether we will be SAVORING the world or SAVING it.

Do we do our assignments RIGHT NOW, in THIS HOUR? Or do we play another round of computer games?

Do we prepare for SAT tests that are months away, or do we go to the football game with our friends?

The choice is always ours, and ours alone, and so are the consequences.

One thing I will say, though, is that it's usually pretty hard to relax with major assignments and deadlines hanging over you.

In other words, you usually HAVE to save the world BEFORE you can savor it.

If you feel the clock ticking behind you, it's unlikely that "fun" stuff will be very enjoyable.

There's really no way to savor a time bomb, is there?

First you SAVE the world, THEN you relax and enjoy it.

That's part of what I mean by your time management "rhythm."

The push-and-pull of working and relaxing... neither has meaning without the other.

"Saving" and "savoring" have to take turns, for EITHER of them to be truly meaningful.

And both of them take place on the hourly level more than any other.

Now, moving from the HOURLY to the DAILY rhythms of life in high school, we're obviously going to find that school and maybe sports is our main daily rhythm and accounts for at least 5 out of 7 days of the week.

So I'll ask you to pause the video for a moment and make two quick lists.

First, what are your routines *before* school on the typical school day?

Second, what are your normal routines *after* school lets out?

In high school we often don't have a ton of CHOICE for ourselves most days -

We are locked in schedules and routines, and often at the mercy of the adults around us who drive us, teach us, coach us, pick us up and stuff.

But, even though you can't usually CONTROL your daily rhythms as a teenager, it's still a great time to gather valuable intelligence on yourself

Remember that one of the key rules of time management is to KNOW YOURSELF - and in this case, you have a chance to learn more about your own rhythms, strengths, and weaknesses during the daily cycle.

So, when I ask the following questions, do you know the answer for yourself?

Bust out your pen and paper and see if you can give good answers to each of these:

1. When during the day are you usually most alert and at your smartest? What hours?
2. How much time do you realistically need to set aside for basic needs like eating, commuting, and bathing?
3. When do you usually get tired? Do you have an afternoon or evening slump? When is it?
4. Are you a morning person or a night person, or some in-between type?
5. What time do you typically want to be in bed falling asleep on a school night?

For example, in my case, I'm usually ALERT in the early morning but VERY SLEEPY in the mid-afternoon around three to five PM.

It might just be because of the Texas heat, but I am DEFINITELY prone to feeling VERY tired around that time of day, especially if I've been working hard all morning.

I've learned to just roll with this NATURAL rhythm, since I can't really control it!

This is one of those time-management things I've discovered, acknowledged, and found a solution to through personal journaling.

Journaling at the end of each day helped me SO MUCH when I was trying to figure out my own daily rhythms for the sake of productivity -

Spend 30 days journaling, literally just 60 seconds per evening, writing down the high- and low-energy points of your day, and it will quickly give you HUGE insights into the rhythms of your daily energy that you can use to your advantage.

Now, on a WEEKLY basis, one of the most crucial, rhythm-based questions I'd ask you as high schooler is - how are you using your weekends?

What sort of weekend habits do you have that might make or break you in the long run?

Sometimes I think use of weekends during high school is one of the main factors that separates the top 10% of performers from everyone else.

Why? Well, EVERYONE in high school seems to be insanely busy during the school week - it's only Friday after school, Saturday, and Sunday that offer ANY real free time.

Some kids use the weekends to sleep; some kids use them to get ahead. It's about as simple as that.

And hey - it's not always by choice, either -

I can think of many times my mom and dad MADE me get out of bed on a Saturday to do something useful and productive.

At the time I can't say I really appreciated it - but now looking back I see why they wanted me to use my weekends for something other than sleep and television.

They were watching out for my FUTURE. I was trying to enjoy my PRESENT.

When it comes to YOUR weekends, which end of the spectrum do you fall on?

Are you SAVING the world on the weekends?

Or are you SAVORING the world?

Maybe best of all, try to do both - a well-planned, 50/50 split of HARD WORK and AWESOME FUN every weekend, is one of the best ways to get the most "bang for your buck" from your weekend time.

I think you should use a moment of each weekend to PLAN the fun stuff you'll do on the NEXT weekend.

Then you can just focus on "hanging on" through each busy school week and making it to the weekend, where you will not only GET AHEAD for next week and reduce your stress...

You'll also have something SPECIFICALLY fun to look forward to at the end of each week.

Remember, an even 50/50 split of fun and work is ACTUALLY going to put you FAR ahead of most high schoolers who are frankly, pretty tired and/or lazy by the time the weekend arrives.

The average high schooler does a typical mix of about 80% relaxing and maybe just 20% work on a typical weekend so it doesn't take that much for you to get ahead each week, I promise!

So, what do you do by CHOICE early on weekend mornings?

Do you still get up early like it's a school day?

Is there still something MOTIVATING and DRIVING you to get out of bed on the weekend?

When you find that thing, you'll get powered up.

I know for a FACT that I routinely jump out of bed at 7 or 8 am even on Saturdays and Sundays by CHOICE because I want to get ahead in business, music, and motorcycling.

No joke, and I'm NOT crazy.

It's EASY to get up when you have something you care about to get working on.

Then, sleep seems BORING in contrast.

That's my key tip for control over your weekend rhythms in high school.

Now, MONTHLY rhythms in high school largely tend to take care of themselves, since the weeks roll by so darn quickly.

Still, it's worth asking yourself in advance: What medium-sized HW assignments, tests, or projects will require a weeks or more of preparation?

And, what will be the highest-stress months of the year?

Is it possible you could think through your schedule, predict those busiest calendar months in advance and maybe plan for them a bit extra?

Here's another thought - can you meet teachers on a monthly basis, during office hours or after school just to check in and show some interest?

Are there any other MONTHLY rhythms that can easily be added to your calendar?

Use a wall planner to map out the school year in broad sketches for any projects, events or studying that will take between a week to three weeks, because these medium-sized projects and exams will dominate your MONTHLY rhythms in high school.

Now, when it comes to your YEARLY time-management rhythms in high school, you want to be building your life around your very biggest goals:

Stuff like finals, college apps, SATs and ACTs - and by the way, check out my other online books because we're always adding new stuff to help with the big moments of high school.

You need to brainstorm all the biggest moments of the coming school year and plan literally everything around those things.

Personally, I like to start with your vacations, especially those which could be planned around college visits.

Or, thinking ahead to SAT / ACT prep and verbal skills, you might take a family ROAD trip instead of flying across the country for a ski trip - because it may be easier to study and build vocabulary, and to do extra free reading, in the long car rides.

On the other hand you might get a summer job - or NOT - depending on what your goals for the upcoming school year are.

The right job could be a brilliant resume-booster, OR it could just eat time on your calendar that you could use for something much more impressive and personal.

The point is, you need to PLAN for it all by brainstorming, anticipating, and creating plans A through C so that the BIGGEST key moments of your year are coordinated properly and you have backup plans for any potential disasters.

The WORST thing is if all the cycles of your yearly events and projects align at the same time and you AREN"T expecting it and you DON'T have any plan to manage the stress and all the work.

This much stress will cause you to become "reactionary" in terms of your YEARLY goals like having a good GPA or getting into college - floundering to stay afloat and gasping desperately across the finish line.

Look - it's bad ENOUGH to get behind the curve on a DAILY or WEEKLY basis, but at least you can catch up later on daily assignments with a few great days or weeks of productivity.

But, if you end up floundering on your YEARLY targets like your Junior-year GPA or getting into college, it can really set you back in terms of reaching your biggest and coolest life goals.

Yet at the same time, it never seems all that urgent to sit down and plan your entire YEAR out - which makes the situation deceptively dangerous.

It's the same in so-called REAL LIFE, but even worse:

No one will EVER ask you to sit down and CONTEMPLATE what you want to ACHIEVE with your life - who you want to BECOME - what you want to DO.

The only way to become the person you want to be is to have some kind of habit - some personal routine that helps you decide if the progress of your YEARS is aligning with the LIFE you want.

That's why it's SO important to pause right now, especially in high school, for 10 to 15 minutes and think about your yearly objectives and roughly sketch them in on your big calendar.

There's one more thing I want you to think about in terms of your yearly progress, and this is something that belongs in your journal.

Take a moment to pause and write about the following question:

How will your life change over the new few years, from 9th grade to 10th, 11th and 12th grade, all the way to freshman year of college?

If you've already gotten through some of those years, please stop reading momentarily and REFLECT on how things have changed for you over those years...

Think in terms of your schedule, your time management skills, your stress levels, your long-term and short-term goals, and anything else that this prompt brings to mind.

REFLECT on your yearly and life-long rhythm and ask where you have been and where you are going.

We are not fixed, unchanging personalities. Take time to think about how you've changed in the past few years.

In fact, I have a fun yet profound related exercise you to do after that.

I want you to think back to yourself in 5th grade.

Picture the stuff that made you happy back then.

What did you LOVE to do most - and get super-excited about? What was your personality like?

5th grade is a great year because you're actually surprisingly grown-up - you know at least a little bit about life -

But you haven't taken in all the outside influences of the outside world, like advertising, parents, teachers..

And 5th graders are still very naive in a charming way - they are very direct with their thoughts and deeds in a lot of ways.

So think back to your likes and dislikes in 5th grade.

In fact, I think you should pause your reading again and remember back and brainstorm for 5 or 10 minutes on this - I PROMISE, it's worth it.

Don't worry, I'll still be here when you "unpause"... so go ahead and do that right now!

...

... Did you do it?

It's kind of funny, but I've learned that the kid we were back in 5th grade is often a HUGE window into what we really care about deep down.

This exercise reveals to us aspects of ourselves that are really TRUE -

And although the specific outward expression may change over time, we will always have those traits and motivations within us.

For example, for myself when I was in 5th grade, I loved cool fast machines and stuff like cars and jet planes...

I loved building FORTS with my classmates and doing LEGOS on my own, I really LOVED exploring outside, I loved to read and learn things on my own -

I really liked to explore and work and learn on my own and I was very independent.

And you can see EXACTLY how this all has manifested in my life now that I'm 28, and that's like 16 years later, because now motorcycling and going fast is one of my favorite hobbies, and particularly all the legos and fort-building has returned in the shape of my entrepreneurship and business-building!

Which is a LOT like getting my classmates to work together and build a fort in 5th grade, surprisingly.

Now bring it back - how could I have done a better job for myself of figuring all this out about myself EARLIER and maybe trying my first business idea a few years sooner?

Because I never GOT the advice I'm giving you now, there was no reason at the time for me to figure out how 5th grade actually connects to real life.

So I want you to take this very seriously, as funny as the 5th grade idea might sound, because it could save you YEARS of frustration and get you to your ACTUAL personal goals much sooner.

So, this has been an overview of how you might conceptualize different rhythms and levels of energy and momentum from the hourly to the yearly and the lifetime level.

Thanks SO much for reading as I tried to explain some of my "deeper" thoughts on life and time management that I hope will be meaningful to you as a high schooler.

Now like I said at the beginning this might click more with the less rational and analytical type minds and more with the creative and artistic types BUT I could be completely wrong about that and I need your advice!

SO, whether you consider your personality more ANALYTICAL or more CREATIVE, please drop me a line on the Facebook page (www.Facebook.com/LovetheSAT) because I'd really like to know what type you are, what you LOVED in 5th grade, and if you think this chapter makes sense or not.

It makes sense to ME but I might be the crazy one so I need your direct feedback on this to know if it makes sense to anyone else!

Drop me a quick note on what YOU liked most when you were a 5th grader and what you took away from this reading, and I'll see you in the next chapter!

13. PLANNERS AND MULTI-CALENDAR TRICKS (PART 2)

Welcome to part two of our two-part chapter on physical calendars and planners.

This ties in to the previous chapter on high school rhythms, AND ties in to the chapter from the previous section about timeless classic tips on using physical planners and calendars.

I've found that the MORE different types of calendars I have in my life, the better-organized and more-productive and in-control I tend to feel.

So, we'll start off with my favorite. The GIANT WALL CALENDAR:

This is the best way to track YEARLY high school rhythms which means HUGE events.

Things like family vacations, finals, exams and projects, mapping out major deadlines of college apps or SAT / ACT prep.

Sports weekends and big championships. College visits and visits from relatives.

All of these MAJOR yearly events can be marked visually and color-coded on a giant dry-erase wall calendar like the one I use every day in my office.

The calendar I use is the the giant 4-foot dry erase wall calendar from Amazon.

It's a reversible, yearly dry erase calendar that measures 48 by 32 inches.

Because there's just a tiny bit of space on the calendar for each day, I also use what I call "mini-journaling" and my own 1-10 ranking system at the end of each day to track the highlights and how I feel each day -

So I continually learn more about what makes me happy and energetic, which continues to reinforce itself and grow more powerful.

HIGHLY recommended.

Again, just order this 48 by 32 inch dry erase wall calendar on Amazon, it's easy to find.

When it comes to DIAGRAMMING the year on your calendar, I suggest you start by figuring out and predicting the toughest and tensest parts of the year and diagraming them in advance on your wall calendar.

Color code this part; for example, you can use BLUE for finals, GREEN for SAT prep, RED for college apps, ORANGE for sports events - or whatever you like!

Just leave a color-code key ON the dry-erase calendar so you don't forget which color means what.

Doing this kind of diagram helps you avoid unpleasant surprises throughout the year.

In the last couple years of high school, you'll have a LOT to do, but you'll ALSO have some element of control over WHEN you choose to do it throughout the year.

By predicting the busier and slower sections of your school year, you can spread the tough work out.

For example, you may realize that you have a ton of rowing competitions in Fall, and rowing team is really important to you, so you want to participate -

Which might mean you ACTUALLY need to be mostly done with college apps BEFORE most of your friends who AREN'T on the rowing team.

They might not have to attend a giant rowing competition during the busiest college apps season, but YOU might!

That's why you can't just act like a lemming and copy what you see your friends doing.

You are a DIFFERENT person with DIFFERENT goals and a DIFFERENT schedule so it's on YOU to use the giant wall calendar to its full potential to help you get into college or whatever your main goal is.

The other thing you need to use the most in terms of physical stuff is your daily planner.

I really suggest you get something cool or fun to write in - something that reminds you why you're doing all this.

I really LOVE to use cool leather journals, especially ones that I get from my travels around the world.

Now this is a HUGE luxury for me, and by using a nice journal as my planner I'm more motivated to ACTUALLY open it up and use it to get things done during the day.

You could also use a purpose-designed daily planner with color-coded and organized tabs, or you can probably find anything you can image:

Amazon or the local bookstore will offer dozens or HUNDREDS of designs for you to choose from each year.

As an ALTERNATIVE to daily planners, if you like to be a bit more spontaneous and free-flowing, you can also copy ANOTHER one of my favorite tricks.

I use 3 by 5 flashcards to make daily index cards of things to do and I carry one with me at all times to help me stay focused.

Throughout the day I will often update my card by copying things over to a new card -

That's when I decide what I STILL need to do, if I should ADD anything to my list, and if there's anything I can actually IGNORE and drop from my card.

I usually make one card before I fall asleep, for the next day.

That keeps me focused during the morning.

Then I make a new card in late morning, again in the evening, and finally one more for the next day.

Like I said, I'm constantly updating it, and it's easy to carry the current card in my pocket.

I STAR the #1 top priority at the moment, and I CIRCLE up to THREE things that need to be done next in no particular order.

When I finish a task, I cross it off - vigorously. Crossing things off your list is the BEST part!

Sometimes I'll keep one card all day if I'm being really productive, because it's SO satisfying to see a whole index card scribbled-out because I've gotten so much done all day.

It's just a little ego boost to remind myself how productive and efficient I'm being.

Now, I also like to have several "monthly" wall calendars throughout my work spaces in key locations.

I'm talking about the normal 30-day wall calendars with a cool picture on the top half and the days of the month hanging underneath.

In my opinion, this is a type of calendar that's less important for daily use.

That's because, for my MONTHLY calendar, I prefer to use Google Calendar or other free, online solutions that work very well for the purpose.

I highly recommend you do the same since you can check that monthly calendar from anywhere.

But, a physical version of the same thing can be VERY useful for noting key dates, keeping track of passing time to stay focused, and my FAVORITE reason, to have inspiring pictures for your room and homework areas.

I love my wall calendars! They help me stay focused and work hard.

The calendar pictures represent a mix of places I want to go, relaxing scenes, boats and motorcycles which are all some of my favorite things that inspire me.

Believe me, this is SUPER effective for motivation and inspiration.

I also "x" off the days of my monthly wall calendar as I go to remind myself how quickly time is passing and to motivate myself to use each day of the month to the fullest!

Now, moving to the DAILY level, don't forget about the humble HOURLY ALARM.

You can find these on your phone, computer, or any simple timer or alarm clock.

Use these to TRACK and ORGANIZE your free time and study time.

For example, you can self-impose personal limits on anything from Facebook to video games to time on your cell phone.

You can also try experiments in setting limits on your homework completion - which I call mini deadlines - for example, saying you'll finish your reading assignment before a 45-minute timer hits zero.

I use these tricks to overcome procrastination and monitor myself for one of the biggest dangers, which is simply getting off track in the middle of the day and never COMING BACK to being productive until the next day.

A time limit can help warn me that my lunch break has gone on long enough, so to speak.

As always, reflecting at the end of each day in a paper journal is incredibly useful / important.

Do you feel in control of your schedule, able to predict in advance which parts of the day will be busy, which parts of the year will be high-stress?

Or, do you feel slammed around by random changes in your schedule and testing calendar, never certain when the next big grade or test is coming around the corner?

Spend a moment in your productivity journal REFLECTING on how you use calendars to make your life easier, and ask yourself if you could make any easy changes to your system that would put you more in control of your schedule.

So, just to conclude and review this chapter on physical planners and calendars:

- First, be sure to get a giant dry erase, color coded wall calendar to map you major events for the year.

- Carry around a cool daily planner that you love to use, or try using my 3 by 5 flashcard to-do lists.

- Choose a couple monthly wall calendars for your work spaces, with pictures that inspire you.

- Use hourly alarm clocks and timers to track and organize your free time and your study time.

- As always, try use a journal to reflect on how you are doing and document your personal progress.

- Everything is easily available on Amazon.com!

So, do YOU have anything resembling my multi-calendar set-up going on in your life or office?

If you DO, which type do you like the best - using daily, monthly, or yearly calendars - or some mix, like me?

Or, do you feel like you could improve and expand your use of physical calendars?

If so, what are you going to do this year to be better about it?

Leave a quick post on the Facebook page (www.Facebook.com/LovetheSAT) to share your thoughts, and I'll see you in the next chapter!

14. NOTE-TAKING AND HIGH SCHOOL TIME MANAGEMENT

In this chapter we're going over the use of handwritten notes to save time, get better grades, and prepare for the increasing demands of college classes after high school.

(Speaking of, you HAVE been TAKING notes as you read... right?)

Handwritten notes might sound old-school but they're an INCREDIBLY effective way of saving yourself massive amounts of time.

Plus, this is something that's absolutely essential to daily life when you get to college, so it's something you need to be good at BEFORE freshman year of college starts.

After we cover both the *need* to take notes and the *awesome benefits* of doing so, I'll help give some suggestions and methods if you're wondering HOW to be a better note-taker.

This is something I've really come to BELIEVE in, by the way, after my six years of full time teaching with students at EVERY level.

I actually used to HATE taking notes, but over the years my own experiences have *proven* to me that this trick works on ANYTHING, ANY TIME.

From high school through college, in your career and in your personal life and independent personal projects...

In fact just yesterday I was listening to a new song I liked and taking notes on it because one of my projects right now it to become a better music producer and composer!

Anytime you want to learn something - or HAVE to learn something - if you want to save time, you take notes.

I mean every chapter, every class, every reading assignment and science experiment.

Take notes when you want to learn MORE, when you want to learn FASTER, and when you want to REMEMBER more.

In fact, taking notes on YOURSELF isn't even weird - and it has a name, something we've brought up before in this book: it's called *journaling*.

I mean, "take notes" is like a two-word universal message meaning "pay attention." Have you ever stopped to think about what means?

Pause for a second and think about this: "You better be taking notes" essentially means "you better be paying attention."

Do you want to be someone who went through their life without paying attention? I know that that sounds pretty awful to me!

So when should you be taking notes? Pretty much ALWAYS, right?

The great thing is, you HAVE to be in class anyway!

Taking notes adds ZERO time to your day and in fact it saves you a TON of time - you'll learn this if you try it out for a while.

I mean when would you ever want to NOT learn faster and better and retain what you learn for longer?

Listen - you're going to have to do this in college ANYWAY.

There's basically no way at ALL to even do KIND of well in college, without taking notes -

You'll look like a total clown in most respectable schools if you're not paying attention and writing things down!

No one will be holding your hand and checking on a daily basis that you understand yet you will be expected to know exactly what's going on at all times in all your classes.

You might not realize this until AFTER high school and college, but what I've come to see is that all the daily quizzes and assignments and the weekly tests and the teachers CALLING on you all the time in high school is NOT because your high school teachers want to HASSLE you, but because they want to CHECK on you.

Your college professors mostly will NOT do that sort of thing for you because they have SO much going on in their own lives.

In fact, when you get to college, ask a few of your favorite professors out for coffee, and talk to them about how they manage their own time and what they have going on outside of the classes they teach.

Not only will this win you points with them but it will also open your eyes as to how incredibly busy they are!

In other words, High School teachers are focused 110% around you and THAT is part of the reason they can seem kind of pesky and annoying sometimes -

Because they're actually ALWAYS watching out for you and focused on you.

Meanwhile, College Professors are THERE for you but they don't just wait around WORRYING about their students the same way many high school teachers do.

College professors have a full schedule outside of teaching so you might just be getting 25% of their full attention.

Professors generally don't spend nearly as much time checking on your daily and weekly understanding...

And when you combine that with the fact that most college books move two to three times faster than high school books, you'll start to see why I'm so ADAMANT and serious that you MUST have good note-taking skills BEFORE you hit the ground in college.

Otherwise you'll get nailed with the end-of-term final exam and realize that you actually don't have any record of what's been covered in class, and it's basically a NIGHTMARE because you only have a few options at that point and they all suck:

Option 1 is to go begging your classmates for notes.

Keep in mind you probably won't know them NEARLY as well as you know your high school classmates...

So it's hard to know at the last minute WHO to ask, WHERE they are at the moment, and IF they will be so incredibly nice that they'll share their semester-long binder of notes with a student that they PROBABLY see as a competitor for grades.

Option 2 is go beg your teacher for notes.

You can try and track down your teacher the day before the test for all the info that you SHOULD have been taking down on your own the past few months of class.

Of book, as I mentioned earlier your teacher or professor will be incredibly busy, plus it's the end of term so it's even MORE busy for them by far, and probably it won't make them too happy if you're banging on their office door pleading for sympathy because you've put in less effort all semester than the top students in their class have.

As a full-time teacher myself I will say I really don't think I would react well to this request for last-second notes because there's not much I can do for you at this point.

You should have checked in with me MUCH sooner and it's also unfair to the harder-working students in my class that I should have to devote additional time to the less-organized students who put less effort into taking notes.

The best thing I could probably do as a professor is hold a big study session for EVERYONE all at one time just before the test, so if this was you as a student you could just PRAY that your professors will do something like hold a study session and that it will be ENOUGH for you to do well on the upcoming test.

My experiences personally suggest that you'd be lucky to come out with a B minus using this strategy.

Been there, done that, got the t-shirt - don't want to do it again.

No thanks, I'll take notes the whole way through so I DON'T have to embarrass and stress myself out asking the teacher for help at the last second.

Option 3 if you don't have notes for an upcoming test is Cross your fingers.

This is terrifying because many final exams are worth an insane amount of your whole grade for the semester, and college finals are about usually two to three times more important and more difficult than high school finals are.

Now, each of these (bad) options could also be said to apply in high school.

But, the stakes are higher in college and there are less guardrails.

You'll find that what you could "get away with" in high school will no longer work for you in college.

So, even though you can "get away with" not taking notes in high school, it's something you'll pay for anyway in college.

Well, not to be TOO doom and gloom - what are some other positive upsides to note taking?

Well let's hit the highlights that occur to me, and I'm sure there are many others:

- Your memory and recall go up
- You'll actually learn more and remember more details for the rest of your life
- It takes less time to study for tests and quizzes
- You'll feel less last-minute panic
- Every homework assignment in class gets easier and faster
- Any pop quizzes will help you instead of hurt you
- You have better study material for major tests and finals

- You can use notes to build up goodwill with other students
- You can lead study groups for additional benefits
- Your teacher gets a better impression of you

Best of all, with a binder-full of notes you'll never have to *beg* classmates or teachers for help and instead can approach them as equals.

So, what about the specific METHODS of taking notes?

Well, it's not hard. If anything, most students tend to OVERTHINK it and OVERESTIMATE the time commitment this will require.

First off all, make sure you have something good to take notes in and it should incorporate some kind of simple organization or filing.

Whether you use durable spiral notebooks, 3-ring binders or a laptop, make sure it's durable!

We've already talked about the importance of good materials and calendars when they can help enhance your time management.

Personally, I think taking written notes by hand is the best method overall.

Its the most real-time, it allows a free-form style for your note-taking and it also connects your brain to your body through your arms, hands, and eyes, which believe it or not tends to increase your memory.

However, taking notes on a computer or some other device does have a few advantages over hand-writing them: it's definitely fast, and the data is more durable if you backup.

Also, your notes will be easily searchable on a computer!

You might be able to find apps that help you take notes, alarms to remind you to write stuff down, or other hacks to enhance your note-taking.

On the other hand, you can do most of this stuff just as easily by hand and you have even more control when working in "the real world" than when you're working through electronics.

When it comes to some kind of organization system for your notes...

The classic is using Roman Numbers I, II, III, et cetera for the BIGGEST sections, and Capital Letters A, B, C, underneath those for major sub-headers within each section.

Under that you do normal Arabic numbers 1, 2, 3 and so on for key points under each main header.

Often times, people who use this system will INDENT each sub-point further and further into the page so that there's kind of an upside-down "tree" of information with each main header having multiple small branches of info underneath it:

    I.   The Roman Empire
        1.   Most important cities
            1.   Rome
            2.   Pompeii
        2.   Major characteristics
            1.   Far-Reaching
            2.   Wealthy
            3.   Well-Armed
        3.   Downfall
            1.   Major events
            2.   Possible causes?
                a) Political/Military?
                        •   Visigoths?
                        •   Internal power struggles?
                b) Lead pipes?
    II.   The Greek Empire
        1.   Critical innovations
            1.   ETC...

You can ultimately use mini bullet-points for any tiny details that belong underneath each key point.

This organizational method works really well because it's simple and natural, plus it's worked for many other students in the past.

There are no real disadvantages other than the need to move quickly as the chapter goes on because this CAN take a lot of time if you let yourself go down the rabbit hole of deeper-and-deeper, super-specific notes.

Try to avoid that and hit key points for reviewing later.

If that system is a little too "rigorous" or tightly-organized for you, try coming up with your own system!

Try to incorporate a system of organization since this will help you remember more.

A few other ideas are using COLORS for color-coding, in the form of highlighters or sticky tabs to mark multiple important spots in a textbook.

Many students also take notes directly in their books, which is incredibly efficient -

Although it means you probably can't sell that book to the bookstore for as much money later, at the end of semester.

Taking notes INSIDE the book or textbooks is actually one of my preferred methods since it's so convenient and fast - but, there's not a whole lot of space to work with so you have to be efficient.

In just about any note-taking situation, you'll need to develop a personal shorthand over time that saves you time and effort.

This can be abbreviations, organization, or the materials you use to take notes.

As you practice your note-taking skills, you will naturally get faster and better at finding the most important info and cutting through the fluff.

Finally, don't tune out of class or reading just because you're taking notes.

You need to split your attention 3 ways: Listening to your professor and classmates, understanding what they're saying, and taking notes on the most important points.

It's a difficult balance that takes practice, effort, and constant attention - but you will be REWARDED for your efforts with less study time AND higher grades.

If you're ever not sure what to write about, just raise your hand and ASK your teacher or professor what the most important points to note down would be.

This will help the rest of the class and make you look smart and interested AND give you better notes to work with.

Plus, when test time comes around, everyone in the class will want your advice and you can earn a lot of goodwill with your classmates.

To review: Note-taking SEEMS like it takes more time, but it actually SAVES you time.

Since you're in class already, it doesn't add ANY extra time to your schedule.

It's like, you have to do the reading assignement anyway, so you might as well take notes so you don't have to read it a second time when you realize you don't remember anything right before your final exam.

Keep things organized and in some kind of durable filing system.

And, never "tune out" the chapter just because you're taking notes. Remember to ask the professor all your questions and don't just get caught up writing non-stop.

If you take notes, you'll rapidly find yourself in the top 10 to 20% of students.

Promise me something - just TRY IT OUT - you have nothing to lose. And it may change your life.

Do YOU take notes in school already? Has it worked for you so far? What sort of methods do you have that work well for you?

Take a moment to pause and leave your best advice on note-taking on the Facebook wall (www.Facebook.com/LovetheSAT).

And, if you have any questions about note-taking for me or your fellow students, go ahead and ask them now on Facebook!

I'll see you in the next chapter.

15. THE ART OF USING FLASHCARDS TO SAVE YOURSELF TIME

In this chapter we're going to discuss the art and the science of using flashcards to save yourself time, increase your memory and reduce the effort it takes to study and learn new concepts in ANY subject.

Flash cards are a NATURALLY-effective, super-simple and super-cheap system that every serious student should have in their study arsenal and they should practice it REGULARLY any time they need to memorize specific "bits" of information like vocab words or formulas.

In a way, making handmade flashcards is simply a continuation and deepening of the art of note-taking.

Flashcards simply distill your notes down even further and further -

They represent the ultimate reduction of critical class information into simple slices and individual, bite-sized concepts that you can quickly drill and memorize before moving on to new topics.

Now, not to brag on myself to much, but remember that I was technically a pretty high-achieving student in high school and college in terms of my grades, my tough classes, near-perfect SAT scores and attending one of the most selective colleges in the world.

I'm only bringing that up right now because I found flashcards incredibly effective in my OWN high school and college experience for the exact same reasons I'm asking YOU to use them now.

I think flashcards are kind of the "pushups" of the academic world.

Like doing pushups, they don't take much time, no special equipment is required, and you can do them anywhere in the world, but they can make you super-buff in surprisingly short period of time.

Also like pushups, flashcards aren't exactly most people's favorite thing, but once you get over the hurdle of doing a few, it becomes an excellent way to build more strength - easy, simple, fast, and free.

As of this moment, I believe the single most concentrated way of rapidly memorizing new information is creating and drilling your own personal set of flashcards.

So HOW can you use flash cards and when are they most effective?

First of all: make new flashcards whenever you have vocabulary words or specialized terms.

You can use them for anything from new English words you're unfamiliar with, to Spanish, French or even Japanese language studies.

Also, specialized terms in class with a simple definition, like "laissez-faire capitalism" or "the treaty of 1842," make excellent flashcards.

The second use of flashcards is to memorize important formulas and equations.

I've noticed that a lot of students don't use this trick and so they struggle on and on for years because they never committed a few simple triangle or circle formulas to memory.

This can work in physics, geometry, algebra, chemistry, calculus, and even music theory.

Third, you can make flashcards of names and dates.

This works for history, english, literature, and other verbal-based and reading-based classes.

Make flashcards for events, characters, and historical figures that you're studying.

Select what you think are the most important three to five facts to recall for each topic and drill them with flashcards.

You'll be amazed how much more this process helps you understand in class, and you'll naturally find it quicker and easier to review for quizzes, major tests and finals.

What about where to GET the flashcards?

Is there a secret, recommended list or some company that makes the best ones?

Or, a specific smart phone app that will allow you to vault ahead of the competition?

Well, NO, there aren't - and that's both a good and a bad thing.

The honest and time-tested truth is that the best way, BY FAR, is to CHOOSE what cards to make, and to make your own cards, BY HAND.

Look, it's really not hard!

It just takes a little time and effort to get the info down on a stack of blank three-by-five index cards.

Don't try to overcomplicate this simple, but time-honored learning tradition.

It may not be a lot of FUN, but think of all the fun you can have with the TIME you save in the long run!

Think of how much less STRESS you'll carry when you just KNOW the material for even the HARDEST classes!

And, think of your excellent grades and test scores so you get into the best colleges and then have even MORE fun!!

Also, if you make the physical flashcards by hand, you can do cool enhancements like color-coding, or little picture doodles that you can use to remember things about the flashcards you've just made.

And, if you want a bunch more tips about how to make effective flashcards as well as how to think outside the box about how to learn vocabulary words more effectively...

Then make sure to check out my other books and online courses at www.LovetheSAT.com, particularly the one called **Conquer SAT Vocabulary,** because this is a topic I go in-depth in for that course.

And in that course one of the many techniques I cover is how to use my simple "2-stack method" to keep your flashcards organized and not waste any time.

The "two stack method" is really simple, which is why I love it. Let me give you the rundown real quick.

One stack of your handmade flashcards is the "daily stack."

You keep between 10 and 20 cards in your daily stack and drill them.. you guessed it, every day.

Each time you feel you've memorized a "daily" card, you get to put it in the "weekly stack."

Then, you GUESSED it again, you review the WEEKLY stack each week on a set date - typically Saturday or Sunday.

Now here's the cool part - any time you FORGET a WEEKLY card during your review session, you take it back to the DAILY stack.

And, if you go over the limit of TWENTY daily cards because of this, you stop adding new daily cards for a while until you get the DAILY stack back below that number.

Ok - so if this was unclear, please rewind and take notes! OR, better yet, ask your question on the Facebook page (www.Facebook.com/LovetheSAT) .

The two-stack method is super-simple -

Actually it's the MOST simple and effective program you can use to ensure a mix of repetition and novelty WITHOUT having to keep track of detailed information...

Other than where you last put your two stacks of flashcards!

Make SURE you keep your flashcards organized by subject and semester, because these make an INCREDIBLE resource for lightning-fast review sessions when major tests and finals arrive.

And when it comes to the subject of how much TIME to spend on flashcards?

NEVER underestimate what you can do with 5 minutes per day.

Fifteen minutes per day is about right for a fairly serious student who wants to go to a great college.

If possible, you can try going up to 30 minutes per day of hardcore flashcards for LIMITED spans of time or upcoming testing seasons.

This type of focused study is VERY intense, but high-repayment -

Whether you are cramming or studying for the long-haul, it will still be one of the most effective study tricks in your arsenal.

Also think about the TIME OF DAY you will do your flashcard studies.

If you're SERIOUS about it like I am, you'll probably find that you get the best results by sticking to a predictable routine.

For example, study fifteen minutes of flashcards right after school on Monday through Thursday, before your other homework.

Take Friday off, then spend 15 minutes on Saturday and 30 more on Sunday reviewing the week's flashcards.

What I've just described is an extremely simple, effective, and fast routine that will find you BLASTING ahead of your previous levels of study skills.

If you're not already incorporating flashcards into your study methods, follow that simple weekly recipe and you will discover how useful they can be for YOU.

A final thought as we wrap up:

When it comes to managing time in school, it's often about memorizing the most information in the shortest, easiest way.

Flashcards, although they're a bit "dry" by nature, are the perfect way to do just that.

Now, I want you to think about a time in the past when using flashcards REALLY helped you study - a class or quiz (or something else) when you used flashcards EFFECTIVELY.

It could be a language class, a math class, or something else.

Go ahead and describe that experience on the Facebook wall (www.Facebook.com/LovetheSAT), because I want us all to share and build up our confidence and understanding of the VALUE of using flashcards.

Finally, if YOU struggle with memorizing important words or info in your high school classes, don't forget to check out my other books and online courses on our website like **Conquer SAT Vocabulary** for more tips and strategies!

You can always find my books and online courses at www.LovetheSAT.com (day or night!)

Take a moment to leave your flashcard experience on Facebook and check out my other video books while you're at it, and I'll see you in our next chapter.

16. ADVANCED HIGH SCHOOL HOMEWORK-MANAGEMENT TRICKS

Welcome to the chapter on additional, advanced, and bonus homework management tips.

The point of this chapter is to include a few more tips that might not deserve a whole chapter to themselves, but definitely deserve a mention as we go on.

Tip number 1 is to "Get Good at Prioritizing."

Each year in school you'll have higher and lower priorities, but as always, the central time management rule of "Know Yourself" applies and helps you sort things out.

If you first know your END-game life priority, you'll have a much easier time establishing what's IMPORTANT and what's merely URGENT.

If you DON'T feel like you know exactly what you want to do yet, then at least know your strong and weak subjects, know your teachers, and establish these strong and weak points early in the year.

Then, as the year goes on, continually develop your ability to rank your assignments by priority in terms of which will have the biggest impact on the things you care about.

It's all about your personal system of ranking important work vs busy work, complex projects vs simple ones, difficult goals vs easy ones, and important long-term dreams with urgent daily concerns.

By this way, this is just one MORE reason for daily productivity-journaling - to reflect on how you're doing and whether or not you could do a better job.

With time you'll naturally figure out what goes where.

Tip number 2 is "Sometimes you're going to come up late."

From homework to test prep - sometimes you might just not be ready on time.

It happens to all of us! And, it's ok, but what are you going to do about it when it happens?

If you're going to be late with an assignment, I've learned that it's best to A) be HONEST and B) let people know as SOON as you'll be late.

The worst they can say is, "no, the original deadline and penalties still apply."

See, you're no worse off than before!

And if you're lucky, they'll find a way to bend the deadline for you.

Don't spend a bunch of time weighing bad options or making up schemes if you're already late on an important assignment.

You need every moment to catch up, so just suck it up, take the small penalties that may be involved, and let your teacher know right away with full honesty because they MAY be willing to help you or give advice.

After all, your teacher WANTS you to succeed in their class - I promise.

Treat them with honesty, and give them advance notice and you may be very surprised how well they react to bent deadlines.

By the way, this is one of many little moments where making friends with the teacher BEFOREHAND can really help out -

They'll be more inclined to stretch the rules and deadlines on your behalf.

Tip number 3 is about using study halls and free periods.

Never forget the impact a free period can have on your schedule.

This ESPECIALLY applies at the beginning of each school year when you're signing up for classes.

It can be a really smart move NOT to over-cram your schedule, and instead leave ONE free period in there for flexibility and backup homework time.

On the OTHER hand, PLEASE do not fall for the age-old trap of thinking that hanging out with friends on campus is more important than school - otherwise known as "more free periods equals better."

Colleges will NOTICE your slacking attitude and you'll pay for the lazy approach to education LATER.

Please - make wise use of the majority of your study halls and free periods to get ahead on schoolwork.

Also - if any of your teachers have an off period at the same time, it's the perfect time to get to know them a little better.

Check the faculty schedules, ask around and see if you can help out any of your favorite teachers or coaches while you're on campus during your free periods.

This kind of stuff pays off in unexpected ways, from the previously-mentioned deadline extensions, to teacher recommendations for college and so on.

And tip number 4 is: Make friends with your teachers!

Being friends with teachers plus gathering a great reputation as a dependable, personable, on-time student will win you MUCH greater chances at leniency when you REALLY need it.

I'm going to tell you a REALLY hush-hush secret - as someone who spent 6 years as a full-time teacher:

Even though teachers KNOW when students are kind of "trying" to impress us in class, we still love it - because it reminds us of why we love to teach and makes us feel like we're doing a good job.

And that's something EVERYONE wants to feel when they're at work!

So, as long as you don't overdo it too much, it's *definitely* a good thing to be an active and friendly participant in classes and to make friends with your teachers.

Now tip number 5 is: Realize when it's time to panic.

This tip, while a bit more dramatic, definitely has the ring of truth to it.

There are some times in life when you just have to drop everything, shut the door to your work area, and not do anything fun until your important work is complete.

I say "panic" half-jokingly, because it's never good to just freak out and freeze up like a deer in the headlights,

But what I mean is, if you're getting that tight-chested, adrenaline-rush feeling of fear, anxiety and panic that you're NOT doing something you should be doing...

...Then my advice is GET OFF YOUR BUTT AND DO THAT THING!

Also, don't tell yourself that it's too late to start.

It's NEVER too late to make a difference.

Tip number 6 is to master the many uses of flashcards.

I've said it before, and I'll say it again -

No matter what technology we devise on our phones and personal computers, the process of making and drilling your own flashcards on key concepts is going to be the FASTEST way to study in virtually any class.

Until we can directly inject knowledge into our brains, I expect flashcards to remain in the top three most effective speed-studying methods.

Tip number 7 is that your own handwritten notes have a *million* uses.

Taking notes on your classes and reading assignments will increase your memory, save time on your study sessions, improve your grades on tests and finals, minimize stress from pop quizzes, make you look good to teachers and win favors with fellow students.

Notes might SEEM to take more effort now than just passively following along, but you'll save HUGE amounts of time later since you won't have to review as much PLUS you'll perform better, so it's a two-for-one win and that's what it's all about.

Speaking of notes, my eighth and final tip for this chapter is:

Review and take notes on this book once or twice a year since you own it for life...

Your perspective on this material will continually change as you grow up and go through more years of school.

If this IS your second or third time reading this book, please leave a special note for us on the Facebook page about what you've learned over the years!

So, those are 8 of my top "quick tips" for homework, school, and time management.

None of them will completely change your life on their own, but taken all together they make a large impact in a wide variety of situations.

What extra time management tricks do YOU think belong on this list?

I REALLY want to know your best suggestions for other tips and tactics that could go with these eight tips.

Leave your ideas on the Facebook wall (www.Facebook.com/LovetheSAT), and check out what other students have come up with!

When you're ready, I'll see you in the next chapter!

17. CREATING YOUR PHYSICAL WORKSPACE

In this chapter I want to cover something that is FREQUENTLY neglected in the lives of many high schoolers and that is to CREATE a dependable SPACE to be productive in.

Ideally, this space is QUIET, CLEAN, and WELL-ORGANIZED.

It contains the MINIMUM-POSSIBLE amount of DISTRACTIONS.

Also it's a COMFORTABLE space that offers possibilities for both SERIOUS and CASUAL levels of focus so that you can use it for anything from light personal reading to the most intense work on your college apps.

This space should be somewhere CONSISTENT that you have CONTROL over, so that you aren't at the mercy of other people, groups, or powers that could stand in the way of you having a peaceful place to work whenEVER you need it.

You need CONTROL over this space so that you can prevent noise, intrusions from other people, and all sorts of other interruptions and distractions.

Why does your workspace matter to time management?

Well, a clean and well-organized workspace typically means that you'll get your work done easier and faster.

With less time lost on distractions, you can commit more energy and focus towards your work and get it done more quickly.

And, the simpler and cleaner you KEEP your workspace, the less time you'll need to spend cleaning and organizing it.

When coming up with my workplace, I like to actually have a two-in-one sort of situation.

What I like is if I have TWO comfortable spots to work in my room - one is "serious," like sitting in a chair at a desk, but still comfortable, and the other is "casual," like sitting on the floor, bed, or a bean-bag chair.

The point is to be able to change it up on a moment's notice so you can flipflop between serious and casual styles of work to suit your mood.

You also want your entire workspace to have the MINIMUM possible amount of stuff so that it's easier to keep clean and organized, which in turn means less time spent looking for things you need.

What's the minimum amount of stuff to be effective?

Well, it will depend on each situation and assignment, but you'll probably need your books or textbooks, your notebooks and writing utensil to take notes, and some form of time keeping and calendar.

If you study well to music, you can also listen to music on headphones, especially concentration-aiding atmospheric music without a lot of words or lyrics to hold your attention and distract you.

Other than what I've just listed, all the electronics, computers, instant messaging, social media distractions, and stuff like that are probably NOT helping you increase your productivity so do your best to get it OUT of the room!

For most teenagers, you simply can't even IMAGINE how much harder it is to sit down and focus these days, compared to how much easier it used to be even just a few years ago.

Most of this new distraction is due to technology, and I think you already know the major culprits:

Internet, cell phones, social media, laptops and computers and video games everywhere, high-definition, on-demand TV, music and movies, instant streaming entertainment...

I'm like, actually SCARED that all this technology is doing more harm than good sometimes.

I mean, I know how much time it saves, and how cool it is to have all this high-tech stuff around, and how amazing our entertainment is these days, but sometimes I'm just worried that I just can't FOCUS anymore!

Personally, I have to make a HUGE effort not to let technology steal all my time, and that means I have to DELIBERATELY CHOOSE to control myself during "work time" even when I have movies, friends, and video games literally at my fingertips.

This may be one of the biggest challenges of time management in the twenty-first century!

So, in your workspace, be sure to MINIMIZE technology: only allow in what you need to actually WORK and FINISH your assignments.

You might need a calculator... do you really need your CELL PHONE, though?

You may have to use the internet for research... but do you really HAVE to check Social Media at that moment?

It's really hard to pull your attention back from Facebook, Instagram or other social media once you're already on it - so make the mature decision to forbid aimless internet surfing in your workspace or homework time.

Here's one more cool trick you should also have up your sleeve:

Make sure to have a backup place outside of the house - but CLOSE to you, ideally within walking, bicycling, or a very short driving distance.

I like this place to have a busy or "coffeeshop" style of energy with some tasty snacks and drinks so I'm excited to go there.

You can use this place to change up your personal study routine occasionally, and it can also be a fun place to meet friends and teachers for meetings and study groups.

Although these busy atmospheres definitely introduce an element of chaos and distraction, they will also jostle up your mind into a higher-energy state when you're surrounded by other productive and talkative people doing work and holding meetings.

Beware of the distractions - but as an occasional changeup to your study routine, a busy coffeeshop near your house is a great thing to find.

So, those are my thoughts on creating an effective study space for yourself.

To sum this lesson up:

1. The quality of your workspace significantly affects your time management skills.
2. Keep a dependable, pre-planned place to work that is always quiet.
3. A clean, well-prepared space will help you finish work faster.
4. Control your workspace and minimize distractions in advance.
5. Recognize the dangers of technology and social media.
6. Find a second "outside the house" place to study as well.

Now it's time to stop reading for a few minutes and go set up your own workspace for homework!

When you've straightened up and organized a little bit, and minimized the interference of outside noise and distracting technology, go on to the next chapter. I'll see you there!

18. TECHNOLOGY AND TIME MANAGEMENT FOR STUDENTS

Technology - the ultimate double-edged sword of time management.

It can help, it can hurt, and everything in between.

There's a fine line between "falling behind the curve" like a dinosaur - think of the generation above you - and "overdependence on technology" - which will distract you from your work with ultimately meaningless entertainment.

Modern technology has led to some of the MOST addictive and distracting media, games, and simulations ever created in human history.

It's absolutely no exaggeration to say that it is harder to focus today than it has EVER been in history and although you may have been BORN into this situation, that doesn't make it any less distracting.

Let's talk about the strengths and weaknesses of technology for high school technology and a few specific ways you can use it to help instead of hurt.

I like to see the positive in things, so let's start off with a list of POSITIVES for technology and high school time management that I came up with.

It helps improve our organization with apps and calendars like the excellent and free Google Calendar.

These same apps can provide us with helpful automatic reminders and alarms, as well as maintain ongoing task lists or to-do lists for us - and a computer never forgets.

Automatic reminders are hardly the only beneficial use of computers and phones.

Flashcard apps offer a fast and convenient backup plan to handmade flashcards, and although I'm 100% in favor of the HANDMADE version, I also think IF you do BOTH handmade and digital flashcards you are going to DOMINATE whatever vocab, language, or other info you are studying.

There are plenty of other good uses for all this stuff.

You can use simple countdown timers on your phone or watch, to organize your time into blocks that fit your schedule and energy levels.

You can use free note-taking apps to quickly jot down ideas or important info, that is saved into the cloud so that you can access and edit it later from your laptop, phone, or tablet - no matter what device you originally created the note on.

Word processing programs save us HOURS of time on hand-writing, editing, saving, revisions, spelling and grammar checking, printing, and sharing by email.

Email also offers us near-instant 24/7 communication with a permanent searchable record of everything you've ever talked about.

And in terms of communications technology, I'm probably just scratching the surface of what we'll see in the next few years... but that's not all...

Cameras have become INCREDIBLY inexpensive, tiny, and high-quality so you probably have access to at LEAST one extremely powerful video camera in your life for personal and artistic projects -

That means student-photographers, musicians, movie makers, dancers, models, and actors have an INFINITELY easier time sharing their work with the world.

And I'm not even BEGINNING to talk about how the internet gives you a potential audience of BILLIONS that, just 10 or 20 years ago was COMPLETELY UNIMAGINABLE -

Talk about a time hack!

I mean, love him or hate him, one of the world's most famous celebrities, Justin Beiber, was discovered via a YouTube video, and in a few short years he became one of the richest and most famous pop stars on the planet -

MY point being - how could YOU live an epic life simply by leveraging and using easily ACCESSIBLE modern technology (like great audio/video equipment for cheap) PLUS the millions and billions of people on the internet who are absolutely STARVING for new daily content and entertainment that YOU could create in some of your free time.

We all have free access to YouTube which, I KNOW I don't need to tell you, is a pretty incredibly place and offers a thousand lifetimes worth of ENTERTAINMENT and SHARED KNOWLEDGE.

Speaking of FREE ACCESS, we also have Google, Wikipedia, IMDB for movies, Genius for song lyrics, an infinite public library online, with instant access to almost the entirety of human knowledge.

Someday soon we may have self-driving cars so you can study while you're taking yourself to school!

But, technology isn't just some perfect solution that makes high school super easy, now is it?

Let's get into some of the unfortunate DOWNSIDES of technology that you absolutely must watch out for, because none of us are immune to them.

We are all vulnerable to different dangers, so these are in NO particular order.

Take notes as we go and decide which risks apply most to YOU:

First, technology can be time-wasting. You lose track of how quickly time disappears because of ADDICTIVE designs in the software and systems.

Second, technology is ever-present and that's one of the main reasons it's so distracting - you literally have to make an on-purpose effort to AVOID technology, even temporarily.

Third, overuse of technology and social media can cause anxiety in some people, or other forms of low-level emotional disturbance and tension.

Fourth, there are also physical dangers: you can easily injure your wrist, hand and eyes from long-term keyboard and computer use.

Fifth, technology can have a social cost. The more fun the games, the less time for face-to-face communication and friendship.

Sixth, there's a very real health cost - your web surfing, gaming, and social media eat up time for sleep, exercise and going outside.

And, my seventh downside of technology is that it also can encourage unhealthy habits and diets because you want fast, convenient food so you can keep gaming or surfing.

Like I said, these are in NO particular order but just a list of risks I put together that I thought were really important, from observing myself, my friends and family, and other high school students like yourself.

I also think SOCIAL MEDIA deserves its own special mention because although Facebook, Twitter, Instagram, and other social sites are extremely powerful and awesome in their own way, they are also the EPITOME of the time-wasting, anxiety-creating DOWNSIDES of modern technology for many high schoolers like yourself.

FACEBOOK and other social sites are DESIGNED and ENGINEERED by some of the most brilliant minds on the planet to hold your attention with content from your friends, and sharing with your peer group.

The instant messaging capabilities of these platforms may be cool and fun, but make NO mistake, they are essentially a PLOT to capture and hold your attention so that advertising dollars can be made by the company whose platform you are using.

There are billions of dollars on the line and teams of geniuses working round the clock on this from every corner of the world and I know that's almost HARD to even IMAGINE but as crazy as it is, it's the honest truth.

Basically, genius billionaires are trying to mind-control your attention from an early age so that they can continue to suck dollars out of the brains of you and your friends and families via social media for the rest of your life.

I know it sounds kinda crazy when I put it like that but, I'm an entrepreneur and businessman myself and I've spent a lot of time studying their design and thinking about why it works so darn well.

I'm not saying NOT to use social media, but I think you can tell that I'm warning you to be VERY CAUTIOUS about the amount of time you spend on it, as well as how SERIOUSLY you take it, because comparing our lives to social media lives is absolutely horrible for your self-esteem and confidence.

Remember that most people ONLY show the highlights and best moments of their lives on social sharing and would be absolutely horrified at the idea of sharing anything embarrassing on social media that put them in a BAD light.

Nevertheless we are ALL human and ALL making mistakes and experiencing trials and difficulties and frustrations every day, but it's only natural to put on a good face and try and impress the people around us so that we gain respect and status.

The problem is social media puts this on an INFINITE loop 24/7 and it's causing a TON of anxiety, depression, and tension purely because we're all comparing ourselves to each other every time we log onto our cell phones and laptops and we get HIT with a dose of social media whether we really need that at the moment or not.

Consider reducing your access and connection to social media without completely cutting the cord.

First, this requires documenting how much time you spend on it each week - then start reducing that bit by bit - or just go cold-turkey, or quit completely, to see how it feels!

I've done this myself and I don't regret it for a moment.

Or, perhaps you can choose very specific times each day or each week to check social media and spend some time on it, but don't use it other than those proscribed times.

Or, set a countdown timer to limit the stretch of time you spend on it...

But please think of SOMETHING to prevent the ever-present social media monster from eating you alive.

And always remember, don't let the "highlight reels" of everyone else's life cover up the fact that NO ONE publishes the BAD stuff, the PAINFUL stuff or the EMBARRASSING stuff that they're going through.

You are more than the sum of your social media presence.

Also, beware of overcomplicating and overdependence on technology -

For example, when you can't find your way home from school anymore because you depend on the GPS in your car.

Or, you lose your cell phone and life grinds to a halt because EVERYTHING you need is there (with no backups) from you calendar to your contacts and homework.

So, never underestimate the power of simple methods.

Think about it this way: humanity made it from CAVES to CITIES, *mostly* without any computers except for the last 60 years or so.

We didn't need computers or social media or cell phones or the internet to make it this far. Those things have only shown up in like the last 1% of history.

Pencil and paper (and your own memory) are still just as important as ever - perhaps even MORE important since they give you an edge over everyone who is just expecting to depend on technology.

Technology should ENHANCE your skills, not REPLACE them. Never become overdependent on it.

You can't have the good without the bad...

For example, the power of the cell phone's instant connection, also carries the risk of permenant connection to time-wasting social media and games in the app store.

Your connection also becomes a distraction.

EVERYONE has different "danger zones" with tech - it could be Facebook and friends, video games, music and media, or tv shows and Youtube.

For me the cell phone isn't that big a deal to worry about, but COMPUTER GAMES can be - they're just so ADDICTIVE to me and time will fly by before I realize how long I've been playing.

For you it's probably something different.

We all have different potential time wasters and we ALL have different ways to ENHANCE our abilities and COVER our weaknesses by using technology to HELP us.

So PLAN OUT your personal strengths and risk factors in advance, and you'll remain more in-control of the overwhelming technological landscape than most people.

And, as always, daily personal journaling helps me reflect on my use of technology.

You can try journaling on this during the middle of the day, at the end of the day, or after any time you spend using your cell phone or computer.

There are even FREE APPS available to help you TRACK your wasted time!

For example, I have an app on my laptop and cell phone that knows which programs are "productive" and which are "time-wasters."

For example, it monitors my use of movie players and video games, as well as social media.

On the flip side, my hours in the word processor spent writing this script would register as "productive" time tracked by the app.

At the end of each week, I get an automatic email giving me a breakdown of what I spend my computer and cell phone time on and I can get a more accurate judgement of my REAL productivity level.

Unfortunately, many weeks I find out that I was MORE distracted than I thought I was - but the feedback is helping me get better at controlling the distractions.

I suggest trying a similar tracking app for yourself and hope you will have a similar experience as you learn to bend technology to help YOU, rather than the other way around!

Here's a quick review and a few conclusions to the topic of technology and high school time management:

- Technology is a powerful double-edged sword whose full effects, risks, and potential are still being discovered.

- As a high schooler, you should focus first and foremost on your REAL-LIFE skills and knowledge. You don't need that much high-tech stuff in your life to be a VERY effective student.

- Know the strengths of modern technology. Be the type of person who has sat down and thought about how it will help you.

- Know the DANGERS and personal risk factors of technology. Identify your key weaknesses when it comes to getting distracted, wasting time, or becoming overdependent on it.

- Never let social media overwhelm you. Never waste energy comparing your REAL life to the FRAUDULENT social media lives of others.

- Find and use a really good free calendar program AND a really good time-tracking app that works across all your computers and devices.

My final word is, keep your uses of technology in high school LIMITED to a few key areas where it enhances more than it hurts.

You'll have time to mess with gadgets and software ALL YOUR LIFE and it's ONLY going to get better as we grow up.

So, enjoy being young, enjoy the outdoors, and enjoy your friends and family.

Learn to solve problems on your own and not depend on a computer, calculator, or GPS unit for help.

That way, you can always stand on your own two feet and you'll have more self-control than about 90% of the modern world.

Then when you WANT it, the technology will be there - but you won't NEED it.

Do YOU think I've brought up some fair points about the strengths and weaknesses of technology?

Please share! This is something I'm REALLY interested in because I want us all to be on the CUTTING EDGE together if you're reading this book.

So, before you go on to the next chapter, please PAUSE and use Facebook wall (www.Facebook.com/LovetheSAT) to write a quick note to "the rest of the class."

Tell us if you think technology is more HELPFUL or more HURTFUL for studying and where you think it will all go in the future!

It's an open-ended question because I want you to respond any way that occurs to you.

To tell the truth, I'm a little bit intimidated by how fast technology changes so that's why I'd love some open-ended thoughts from my students on it, since I know ya'll love to stay current on this stuff.

Let me know your thoughts and I'll see you in the next chapter!

19. MAJOR PROJECTS, TESTS, AND FINALS

In this chapter I wanted to spend a little focus on one of the most INFLUENTIAL elements of high school and pre-college readiness. I mean the major tests, final exams, presentations, and large projects that heavily affect your grade in most classes.

Planning and preparation are required when it comes to your biggest projects for the semester, or you will be tumbled around at the mercy of events - and will also get lower grades in addition to being more stressed the whole time.

AND, you're missing your chance to get ready for college by rising above the level of the average high school student and learning to work really hard and solve big problems.

So, how does a top student go about preparing for the biggest grades of the semester?

Is there any way to control the major events of the year, or are you at their mercy?

Often, these types of assignments and tests can be 20%-30% of your final grade for a book in high school, and in college this may increase even more -

Sometimes up to FIFTY percent of your entire college-class grade for the semester can be riding on a single giant test or project.

So here's a bit of intimidating news, and it might be something you already know from bitter personal experience:

One bad test or major project can RUIN your overall average.

See, one thing I slowly realized is that when it comes to your overall grades in high school, the daily mini-quizzes usually are MUCH less important than the occasional BIG grades.

HOWEVER, I *also* eventually realized that the daily mini-quizzes are like a WEATHERVANE of how I'm going to PERFORM on the day of the big test.

What this all means is that it's ALWAYS smarter to study for something BIG than something SMALL.

And, if you're in a particular time crunch, it's OK to get a low grade on a tiny quiz the next day, if that buys you time to study for a giant exam, and the same rule goes for college.

BUT, you have to pay CAREFUL ATTENTION to your daily, minor grades on quizzes and small homework assignments.

It's not so much about the POINTS themselves as what the scores are TELLING you...

Because, any class where you are getting a series of low DAILY grades, you are 100% for sure BEHIND the curve when it comes to the big test. That's just how it is.

Like I said, COLLEGE is like this too, only even MORE - the final tests and projects are HUGE, and there's not much daily work to make up your grade if you screw up majorly on the big stuff.

Now, not to make a point that's TOO obvious already, but my favorite study tactics of NOTE-TAKING and SELF-MADE FLASHCARDS come to the rescue again by saving you time later on when you have to study for finals and major tests.

Like many of these rules, this is something that's going to also go DOUBLE for college.

And, by now you KNOW that I really want you to be ready for college and an awesome life beyond that.

So, here are six of my best quick tips for dominating MAJOR grades like exams and major projects.

Tip number one is USE THE SYLLABUS.

One of the easiest and most overlooked tips is to NOT LOSE THE SYLLABUS that your teacher gives you on the first day of class and actually to USE it unlike most students!

Not only should you preserve each syllabus with your life, you should also make digital copies as WELL as commit it to your major personal calendars in the first week of school.

I mean, talk about a CHEAT sheet for time management!

If you follow my advice and put it up on your yearly calendar, you'll have a color-coded wall calendar for the entire school year, marked with all your major tests, projects, and finals for each class.

It will be a visual guide to the quicksand of high school - where 99% of students just stumble through events and assignments, you will have a birds-eye map to help you through the journey from day one.

Plus, checking the syllabus FIRST makes you sound MUCH smarter when you move on to tip two, which is:

Ask the teacher.

Once you've gone over and mapped out the syllabus on your own, you'll be in an incredible position to have a smart discussion with each class teacher about what the most difficult sections of their class tend to be.

Where are the biggest assignments that cause the most trouble for students each year?

You can literally just ASK your teachers and most of them will be able to give you some excellent advice.

It only takes three to five minutes of their time and you can usually catch them after school if you let them know how interested you are.

Remember, this is by FAR the most effective if you do it at the very beginning of every semester.

Then again, although they WANT to help, teachers aren't always the most accurate judges of the difficulty of their own tests and homework assignments, so tip number THREE is:

Ask the grade above you.

The kids in the grade above you can ALWAYS tell you what the hardest stuff will be for the upcoming year.

Juniors will know what to warn sophomores about, sophomores can show freshman the ropes, and so on.

If you're on a sports team or any club, for example, that's a great place to ask around.

Keep your ear to the ground - what are the big projects, classes, and tests that the older kids fear?

Give yourself a heads-up - those are the events to mark with a red star on your yearly calendar.

Tip number FOUR is to monitor your "small grades."

Like I mentioned earlier, you CAN afford to bomb a FEW small quizzes or daily assignments IF you are putting that time into other MAJOR grades and IF you only do this in the most desperate situations.

HOWEVER, if you experience a string of bad daily grades, that is an extremely worrisome trend that MUST be corrected immediately or you will face serious punishment and possible disaster on the next major grade in that class.

This is a virtually unbreakable rule so, no matter how much you want to bury your head and ignore a downwards trend in your hardest and least favorite class, you simply CAN'T afford it because when a big grade shows up it will already be too late.

Tip number FIVE will definitely help with the previous problem, and it's to keep an incredible calendar at home.

Use your YEARLY, MONTHLY and DAILY calendars to organize visually and in places that you'll see REGULARLY.

You can also use long-term reminders on your digital calendar to give you reminders MONTHS from now - so at the beginning of the school year, you could set a calendar alarm to go off in November and send you an automatic email or alert you that it's time for college apps or to start studying for SAT prep.

Hopefully you can also get your hands on one of those giant 4-foot dry erase wall calendars with color-coding like I keep recommending. Go back over both chapters on physical planners and calendars to help you hack your school year.

My final quick tip is to start preparing early, and never stop preparing.

It's like a zombie apocalypse - until you're out of school, the tests and projects will just keep coming no matter how many you kill.

And then, you get to real life and the work world and you realize, to be successful, it's the exact same thing.

It's never over. Life never quits. The tasks and demands just keep coming.

The endless summer is never here, and honestly, even if it WAS, you would get bored as heck two weeks in.

So learn get the most, to MAKE the most, out of every minute.

When I'm not being productive, I try to ask myself during the day:

"Am I really ENJOYING myself right now, and I really RELAXING, or am I just being bored and lounging lazily?"

If I'm not REALLY enjoying myself or REALLY relaxing, then why am I not working on a major project? WHY am I not working towards my dreams? Since I KNOW what I want to do with my life - ride motorcycles, make music, and start awesome businesses - It seems boring to me to be lazy.

I want an EXCITING life, not a RELAXING one, and I've realized by now that it takes a daily effort to have one - because exciting lives are MADE, not given.

I know it might seem strange that I'm connecting your giant History paper in high school with having an exciting life after college, but TRUST me - there's a strong connection.

If you can get through the HARD stuff, you earn your way to a lot more of the FUN stuff. I promise. This is just a natural law of success and achievement that operates the same way in high school as it does when we become adults.

Here's a quick review of what we've covered in this chapter on major tests and projects in high school.

- First, use each class's CURRICULUM to plan your year. Then ask teachers and students the grade above you for further advice about the toughest parts of the year.

- Never lose track of the BIG tests and projects in the midst of all the daily details because in the end, the BIG grades almost always ends up counting for much more in the scheme of things.

- Plan things out in advance by researching, using calendars and planners, and staying in touch with your teachers constantly.

- Prioritize the major stuff. Make sure you are set up to do really well on THAT stuff, then do as MUCH of the smaller daily stuff as you can.

- Still, always monitor your daily grades.

- A string of bad daily grades indicates your next major project or test will be extra-difficult for you, but it's never too late to make a book correction in class.

- NEVER be afraid to talk to your teachers after class to explain your situation and for advice on how to recover in preparation for a major grade.

- As always, being HONEST and going to your teacher as SOON as possible is the best way to win a little leniency from them.

Here's my final question for YOU - what's YOUR best quick tip to me and the rest of the class, for dealing with major tests, projects, or essays?

Is it a way of preparing in advance, motivating yourself, setting deadlines, or what? How do YOU do it?

I'd love to know what YOU do to handle and prepare for the toughest assignments of the year, so please leave your thoughts on the Facebook wall (www.Facebook.com/LovetheSAT) and then I'll see you in the next chapter!

QUIZ #3: MIDSECTION QUIZ

Welcome to the third quiz of Ultimate Time Management for Teens and Students!

Remember, it's all about memory and recall.

There's no time limit. Go slowly and try to get them all correct.

Answers are on p.189.

QUESTION #1: My friend "Sam," who has focused on one singular passion since I first met him, now successfully works in what high-competition industry that he studied as a teenager in high school and college?

A) Inventing improvements to cell phones.
B) Racing Motorcycles.
C) Directing Movies.
D) As an SAT / ACT tutor.

QUESTION #2: What is the difference between "saving" the world and "savoring" the world?

A) When you "save" the world you're working hard and when you "savor" the world you're stopping to "actively relax" and enjoy life.
B) "Saving" the world is about improving your community, but "savoring" the world is about being lazy and just enjoying what's going on around you.
C) There's no difference - the idea is that BOTH of these things should always go together with each other!

QUESTION #3: When mapping out your giant year-long wall calendar, you should START by recording and making time for:

A) Daily-level events.
B) Weekly-level events.
C) Monthly-level events.
D) Yearly-level events.
E) Life-level events.
F) None of the above.
G) All of the above.

QUESTION #4: Although taking notes in class is an IMPORTANT and EFFECTIVE way of saving yourself time in high school and college, you must simultaneously...

A) Try to organize your notes as you go.
B) Use a personal shorthand to save yourself time.
C) Make sure you don't stop listening to the teacher just because you're writing notes.
D) Contribute to class discussion.
E) All of the above.
F) None of the above.

QUESTION #5: What is the BEST source of flashcards for most classes?

A) Amazon.com (an online bookstore) has the BEST selection.
B) The local bookstores you visit in your hometown will have EXCELLENT options.
C) Self-selected concepts and handmade flashcards.
D) Phone Apps in the App Store.

QUESTION #6: Which of the following options are making and drilling flashcards ideal for (according to this book)?

A) Quickly memorizing specialized terms and vocabulary, formulas, names and dates.
B) Gaining deeper understanding of math and science practice problems.
C) Doing deep character/plot analysis for English class.

QUESTION #7: When you're going to be late with an important assignment for school, you should...

A) Let your teacher know as soon as possible - they may show leniency.
B) Come up with ANY plausible story that you can tell your teacher so that they won't be as likely to penalize your score - this will help keep grades higher for your college apps.
C) Try sneaking the assignment in on the teacher's desk or in their mailbox - this has worked for HUNDREDS of my students in the past.

QUESTION #8: Why must you maintain CONTROL over your workspace and homework area?

A) You need to feel a sense of power and control in your workspace, since it's SO rare to feel this way during the school day.
B) You need to follow all my rules about time management, regardless of whether you understand them or not - THAT'S why.
C) You need to be able to work in a dependable, clean, and quiet space whenever you need one on short notice.

QUESTION #9: Why is technology the ultimate double-edged weapon for high school time management?

A) Our teachers can use technology to give us better lessons, BUT that reduces the interaction between instructors and students.
B) Social media is a platform for students to share knowledge and create study groups, BUT there's an associated cost for advertising.
C) There are many hi-tech ways to get your work done faster, but you can ALSO get totally distracted very easily.
D) Wikipedia and Google help you research projects quickly, BUT it's easier to accidentally plagiarize your research.

QUESTION #10: Daily quizzes and small assignments are less important than major grades, yet they still matter a great deal because...

A) Daily grades are what will impress your teacher for college recommendations, more than major grades.
B) A string of bad daily grades indicates that your next major test or project will be extra-difficult for you.
C) Daily grades are the first thing colleges look at during the application process.
D) Daily grades are how your parents will keep track of your progress in school, and low daily grades will make them REALLY stressed (leading to extra tension between you and less freedom on the weekends).

ANSWERS ON p.189.

20. MAKING SPACE FOR YOUR SAT AND ACT PREP

Ok, so now let's talk about a topic that's near and dear to my heart: SAT and ACT test prep.

So as you probably learned during the introduction, I happen to know a TON about SAT / ACT prep - like, WAY more than any human should probably know.

The tests have changed a lot over time, but our company and I have always stayed on top of them.

To hit a few of the highlights, I got a 1590 out of 1600 in high school - and since then, I've gotten a perfect score on the official SAT more than once.

I've taught SAT prep full-time for four and a half years, started one company and two blogs around test prep, written 5 textbooks on SAT prep and over 250 related articles in the past five years.

Now, this matters to YOU because hypothetically as a motivated high schooler reading one of my books you are interested in COLLEGE or CAREER SUCCESS or whatever else you want to achieve.

And for MOST of those types of students, like I was, your test scores are gonna matter.

Probably they are going to matter a LOT - influencing everything from who your friends are to what you do for your first job.

Now I try to keep perspective - even as a pro SAT tutor, it's not like your test scores DEFINE you as a person or CONTROL your very life and death -

BUT, test scores are very important to 99% of high-achieving high schoolers.

There's no way around it because of how LARGE the educational system is;

110

there has to be some "quick" way of sorting students by academic performance, even if it's imperfect like SAT / ACT testing.

So if you agree that your test scores are important and you think you can trust me to give some HONEST and WELL-QUALIFIED advice on the subject that I think will help you, then listen up:

First rule - when it comes to test prep, earlier is ALWAYS better - no exceptions.

The SAT and ACT tests are HUGE - comprehensive, intense, and high-stress.

Even a *single* practice test will require upwards of six to ten hours or more to take, grade, and go over for mistakes and corrections.

You can never make new time, AND it's easier to REVIEW than to LEARN.

An IDEAL time to start for most families is the Summer before Junior year begins.

At this point, there is literally NO stress with regards to test prep, and if you make a weekly effort to improve with a tutor or on your own, you are virtually guaranteed a MUCH higher score by the time you're a Senior.

The next-best time to start is Winter break of Junior year - beginning your test prep after you finish your winter finals or after the new year when you're back from Christmas vacation.

Starting then will still give plenty of time to prepare but you will need to be vigilant about your practice because you will find final test dates approaching faster than you expect.

The third best time to start your test prep is in the early spring of Junior year - ideally, before Spring Break, so that you can use some of your vacation time for intensive study.

If you work hard each week, and use the coming summer months, you will still be in EXCELLENT shape to perform your best.

After Spring of Junior year, it's getting late in the game.

For example, here's something you might not have considered:

It's hard to make a serious effort on test prep during the final semester of Junior year, when projects, finals, and activities typically eat your entire schedule as the year comes to a close.

Summer before Senior year offers a LOT of time to study, but only IF you aren't taking part in summer camps, jobs, and hanging out with your friends ever day.

And, you should be doing a ton of work on your college and scholarship apps during this summer.

Furthermore, it is much, MUCH better to be REVIEWING your SAT / ACT prep in the summer before Senior year begins - not learning the material for the *first time*.

Finally, by Fall of Senior year, you're back in the middle of school, and this is typically a very busy high school semester. You don't want the pressure of also HAVING to study test prep hardcore during back-to-school season.

Be SMART about it and plan in ADVANCE.

Please don't be one of those families who comes to me in a panic asking what they can do in 4 weeks to prepare for the SAT and "they have to get 200 points" for their favorite college.

That's dangerous. Don't be that student - plan it out on your calendar, thinking about the BUSY and the SLOW seasons of high school and how to use them to your advantage to accomplish your test prep.

Now, what exactly do I mean when I say "start your SAT / ACT prep"?

First and foremost, I mean to make a plan and hopefully talk to an expert about your situation.

Contact us by email (Help@LovetheSAT.com) or find local tutors or test prep companies because they SHOULD be happy to give you FREE advice about what you need to do next for your SAT and ACT scores.

There's also a lot you can do on your own!

Learn the basics of the tests including which one you'll be taking (or both), the differences, the test dates, and the basics of the curriculum.

Work regularly on your college-level verbal skills starting now. Learn to love your free reading and vocab building.

Also, investigate group-class options in your area for SAT / ACT prep.

Groups are great as introductory and intermediate-level ways to get to know the tests - as long as the instructor and the book are high-quality.

They're not as personalized as 1-on-1 tutoring but can offer an excellent value if you're able to speak up and ask your questions in class without being shy, and if you do all the assigned homework and just generally do everything you can to get the MOST out of your investment in group class.

Otherwise you might unfortunately end up with generic information or info that's not relevant to you - so be sure to HELP your test prep instructor by TELLING them what you need extra help on.

Go deeper and look into private tutoring options around you, or online tutoring, which is something we also offer at Love the SAT!

SAT / ACT tutoring is one of the best ways to get expert help and a good test prep tutor will save you time and energy while also improving your score.

And luckily, the financial investment of tutoring can usually be recovered in a short time through better college and scholarship prospects.

Whether you're in a group class, tutoring, or on your own, it's also incredibly important to work through practice sections of the SAT or ACT.

Taking it up a notch from short practice sections of the tests, you'll also want to include full-length, timed-and-graded practice tests that you take on Saturday mornings like the real thing.

Adding an element of timed pressure makes your practice more authentic and the length of the practice tests helps you build endurance.

Furthermore, your missed questions will provide a valuable source of additional practice and study for your NEXT attempt at a high score.

You can even keep a "test prep journal" to chronicle your efforts and your successes that will also help you self-identify your strong and weak points through reflection and documentation.

Take your practice tests starting EARLY on Saturday morning to replicate the conditions of the official test as precisely as you can from your home.

Tutoring and testing companies near you, like ours at Love the SAT, should also be able to help with practice testing as part of their services or lesson packages.

Of book, the ULTIMATE measure of your readiness is official SAT or ACT testing.

You want to feel prepared BEFORE you try to take an official SAT or ACT, although the very first time might be more of an experiment than a serious attempt at your highest score.

Ideally you want to go through MULTIPLE rounds of this entire process - planning, practice, and testing.

I recommend taking three official tests if possible: Halfway through Junior year, at the END of Junior year, and at the BEGINNING of Senior year.

As you can imagine, this requires a large time commitment which is exactly why I chose to include this chapter in this book.

Although the time commitment is significant, so are the rewards.

Higher SAT / ACT scores are SO competitive precisely BECAUSE of how big a difference they can make - they have VALUE.

If you believe in the VALUE of higher SAT / ACT scores, you have to be WILLING to invest TIME and even MONEY into personal studies, prep materials, and possible tutoring or group classes.

But, one of the most critical "secret weapons" in test prep is just to START EARLY and BE CONSISTENT - this is a guaranteed recipe for better test scores.

The more time you can INVEST to your test prep, the better your final results will generally be.

It's pretty common sense, but for some reason families always need me to point it out - the MORE you study, the better your scores.

Again, one of those SIMPLE and common-sense things that sometimes gets obscured by all the mythology and hype surrounding SAT and ACT scores.

If you're late, just start TODAY by getting your hands on some good books and a good tutor or class.

It's not ideal to get a late start but what matters most is how much time you can commit with the days you have left.

Consider what activities, entertainment or social time can be dropped temporarily while you invest that energy into studying.

Now, there are also some supplemental things you can do that are free or low-cost to boost your scores.

The following ideas can all help round out the studies you do with tutors, teaching, and practice testing.

First of all, you should be reading and building your vocabulary as much as humanly possible. This will pay off for life even after SAT and ACT testing is over and done.

Also get your hands on additional test prep textbooks, workbooks and e-books.

We constantly look for the best books for teens by other authors, so please visit www.LovetheSAT.com for current suggestions from our blog if you want a little more help!

Watch and take notes on online educational videos from Youtube.com and Kahn Academy.

Also check out **our other online courses and books** (which we also host at www.LovetheSAT.com along with the blog and other cool stuff).

I bet they'll prove useful!

Read blogs on SAT and ACT prep like ours at www.Love the SAT.com/blog.

Participate in pre-college online discussion forums like College

Confidential.com and ask peers and fellow forum contributors for advice and help.

And, be sure to contact experts like us by email or phone to see if you can get some extra info from the pros.

So, how are you even supposed to find TIME to do all this work when you're already busy with school and activities?

Test prep requires you to CARVE OUT TIME in your schedule and **stop making excuses for why you're too busy**.

WEEKENDS are great for *dedicated*, full-length practice tests or large chunks of tests to work on your endurance and test-taking.

TUTORING SESSIONS on a regular, weekly basis after school provide a "due date" for your test prep homework each week and offer a second chance to go over and learn from your weekend work.

AFTER SCHOOL but BEFORE you do other homework is generally the best time for 10 minutes of supplemental vocab flashcards - so, before you've done all your other homework, gotten sleepy, and gone to bed without building your vocabulary.

And, AFTER HOMEWORK is done, but BEFORE bed,is ideal for twenty to thirty minutes of extra free reading to put you above and beyond your peers.

Other ideal times for free reading are carpools, bus rides, commutes (with your parents driving) and vacations - particularly the slow and boring "travel" parts like sitting in the airport.

You MAY have to DROP another, more fun activity temporarily while you take test prep classes or tutoring.

Good private test prep is usually not cheap so you need to focus 110% on your teacher and your homework.

You must VALUE a higher score and understand how it fits into your OVERALL plan for your life and goals.

If you still don't believe you'll have the time or energy for test prep, please refer back to the LAWS of time management in the introduction.

If you know what you want out of life, then you'll start to see how the pieces fit together - and that's when you'll gain the energy and focus to do the hard stuff in your free time - like SAT and ACT prep.

The bottom line is that SAT /ACT scores are a matter of motivation, preparation and practice.

A good teacher helps, but the MOST important factor is your own purpose in life mixed with your focus and invested time and effort.

I'm speaking from grim personal experience when I say that it's easy to blow this off and leave it for later, but top students simply FIND a way to study for the SAT and ACT.

I consistently see top students purposefully starting test prep early and continuously carving out time in their week to prepare, regardless of other activities they'd RATHER be doing.

Copy their example. You DO have enough time to study. You just have to USE it.

For more SAT and ACT info, visit us at www.LovetheSAT.com and don't forget to check out our other online video courses, articles and books!

And, if you have ANY questions about test prep WHATSOEVER, now's a great time to ask them via email (Help@LovetheSAT.com) before the next chapter.

Let me just remind you that I'm literally one of the world's top pros in the field of SAT prep - that's not bragging, it's simply true - and I also know a TON about the ACT test...

So, if you've EVER wanted to ask a pro SAT tutor something, now's the time!

It's fun to get the tough questions, so ask anything you're wondering. Send us your questions via email (to Help@LovetheSAT.com) , and I'll see you in the next chapter!

Further Reading:
www.LovetheSAT.com/prepping-SAT-at-home-complete-guide

21. PLANNING FOR COLLEGE APPS AND DEADLINES

In this chapter I knew I needed to hit something that's CRUCIALLY important to almost all high schoolers and it's something that I'm sure gets on your mind more and more as you go from Freshman to Senior year and **I'm talking of course about COLLEGE APPLICATIONS.**

There's also the research involved in SELECTING potential colleges - another part of the process that will take a lot of time and simply cannot be rushed.

Last but not least, you absolutely should explore your SCHOLARSHIP options - more on that in a few minutes.

Basically, the entire process is TIME CONSUMING AS HECK - at least, if you want to do it properly - and you SHOULD - because these decisions are going to affect your life quite a bit!

For example, part of selecting your top colleges includes taking in-person campus tours.

Although we can't always tour every college we want because of limitations on time, budget, and distance, it still pays to see any schools that you can.

And that means, you'll have to give up a lot of time and energy that you COULD use for other things like schoolwork.

My point is, this eats up even MORE free time that you might have expected to use for college apps -

So plan to use some of your breaks and/or long weekends to get out of town and go visit some schools.

Don't be fooled into leaving all your tours for summer.

Although that's a good time when YOUR schedule is not so busy, campus will unfortunately feel pretty dead and it's much harder to get a feel for what the place is like when school is in session.

Campus tours are just ONE of about a MILLION reasons why you MUST start your college application process FAR in advance - months and months before most of your competition begins to work.

By carefully planning and budgeting your time amidst all the other demands in your life, you'll be able to

A) Find some great choices for schools,
B) Craft fantastic applications that win your seat at the best schools, and
C) Massively reduce the cost of your education by winning scholarships and grants.

Now, I'm mainly going to approach this next bit from the perspective of a student who is a Junior or a Senior.

However, everyone should be listening and taking notes because this is the probably the BIGGEST project of your entire high school career.

Even if it's not your turn yet to apply to college, it's still one of those situations where the more you know, the better off you will be.

First, I'm going to try to briefly, (or at least as briefly as possible), summarize the most important tasks, dates, and seasons of the college apps process, mainly for Juniors and Seniors.

It's hard to do a "COMPLETE" list of EVERY last thing you'll need to do for college apps, but I'm going to make sure we hit the highlights and all the important stuff.

Be sure to check the book store or my instructor profile for other video books that will help you with all this stuff in more detail!

I can't make a COMPLETE list of every detail right now, but get your pen and paper ready cause I'm going to hit a LOT of the highlights.

Here we go:

Your first priority must always be your school classes and grades. This is a full-time job and then some. Never sacrifice your grades and good standing in school for ANYTHING!

Take the hardest classes you can without burning out, and keep your good grades first and foremost in your mind at all times.

Up next are extracurriculars, sports, clubs and leadership positions - in other words, your resume!

Obviously these activities take up a huge amount of time for all four years of high school and will be almost as important on your resume as your grades are.

Next in importance come your test scores - meaning the SAT and ACT.

Test Prep should generally start in Fall or Winter of Junior Year and continue all the way through Fall of Senior Year.

Try to plan your test prep for slower seasons of your year;

For example, if you're a huge varsity football player and your team is in the running for the championships, then you know you'll probably have a very busy football season -

So PLAN your test prep to start immediately AFTER the busiest part of your sports season.

Once your grades, resume, and test scores are looking solid, it's time to start researching possible colleges.

This is also known as making your "long list" and should include several weeks of research with books and internet as well as conversations with counselors, parents, teachers, and anyone else you look to for advice.

Winter of Junior Year is probably my ideal time to make a Long List of colleges so you know your specific goals as you come into the very busy end of Junior year.

When you have a long list ready, it's time to gradually whittle down into a refined final list.

You need to use every trick at your disposal to make a highly-targeted and smart final list of colleges you will apply to.

Of book, you should follow the age-old advice of applying to a mix of schools, ranging from "I'm sure I'll get in here" to "wow, that's a big reach for me."

But, each college you apply to means more time spent on college apps, higher application fees, and more stress.

So, you want to use tricks like campus tours, alumni interviews, and hardcore personal research to uncover a list of colleges that fits you perfectly.

You need to finish your college list in time to actually DO your COLLEGE APPS and ESSAYS, because that's the next stage of the process!

This stage probably SEEMS like it takes longer than it really does, because if you work efficiently you can actually make a lot of progress in a relatively short time.

Consider tricks like creating one MAIN resume before you even begin any specific college application -then you can use the resume as a handy reference to fill out all your applications quickly.

Also think about how your essay themes and examples can be adapted to fit multiple college essay topics.

You should never re-USE an essay for two colleges, but you ALSO don't need to keep re-inventing your topics, stories, and themes that you use as the CORE of your best college essay ideas.

Between copying over info and writing new essays, you'll probably want about a week of work time budgeted per college app at a BARE MINIMUM.

Obviously you can rush your applications and finish them in just a few hours, but then you won't have time to edit, get feedback, do your best work and all that good stuff.

So students who RUSH through the stage of filling out college apps will be very vulnerable to competitive students who planned better and spent more time crafting an incredible-looking application.

Make no mistake, this kind of detailed, patient work on your entire college application makes a BIG difference in the impression the application committee forms of you.

And some kids, like I was, are spending a LOT of time carefully making a great application - that's your competition.

Don't underestimate how time-consuming the paperwork and essays can be, and try to leave yourself spare time so that you can find other people to look over your work and help you edit your essays.

By the way, at the same time you start your college apps, you should also be printing out teacher recommendation forms and nicely asking your favorite teachers to fill them out for you.

Go with teachers that LIKE you and whose class you PARTICIPATE IN and CONTRIBUTE to.

It's incredibly important to give them weeks of advance notice because high school teachers are VERY busy and the last thing you want is to have an angry and frustrated teacher writing your college recommendation!

Plus, the earlier you are to ask, the more MATURE you seem - always a good thing when someone is about to write a reference letter on your behalf.

That's almost all - now you just need to send in your apps and wait patiently to hear back.

But don't just sit around... if you're REALLY smart you'll make a plan to win thousands of dollars in college scholarships so that you barely have to pay anything for your education. More on this in a moment!

Now, the entire process I've just gone over basically describes the "average" or "typical" college-app situation.

But of book, NO ONE turns out to be "average" or "typical," so make sure you've considered all the angles and done all your research and planning for yourself.

However, there's one thing that applies to almost everyone: PLEASE DON'T be fooled into thinking its "just seniors" that need to think about budgeting time for college apps and research.

If you start the college process a few months earlier than the rest of the pack, you can USE extra time to win TONS AND TONS of money from scholarships and alternate financial aid.

Don't laugh if that sounds crazy to you, because if you start early ANYONE can do this - there are literally billions of dollars in unclaimed college scholarship money each and every academic year.

So, if you manage your time effectively and get the bulk of your college research, and apps and essays done ahead of time, what I'm saying is you'll have extra time to win the exact scholarships and grants that your classmates DON'T even BOTHER to apply for -

Because they'll all run out of time senior year and be crushed just keeping up with college apps and school.

My way of thinking is, you're going to HAVE to do college research, applications and essays ANYWAY, so really WHAT is the POINT of delaying?

By finishing early, you free up time to get PAID very handsomely for filling out scholarship apps!

I don't think I'm exaggerating to estimate the number of high schoolers who are early-starters on their college apps at just 1 in 1000.

So out of every 1000 high school students, probably only about ONE will start early enough to have time for any scholarships.

So you MAY think you have NO CHANCE at winning any scholarships because there are "so many better students out there" -

But the thing is, EVERY high schooler basically says this to themselves, and then everyone runs out of time Senior year, just trying to stay afloat with school and college applications -

So I'm saying out of every THOUSAND kids who COULD apply for a scholarship, NINE HUNDRED AND NINETY-NINE will NOT apply for even a SINGLE scholarship just because they're running out of time and they don't believe in the odds anyway.

That's not just the "lazy" kids, it's also highly-competitive kids like MYSELF who don't apply for any scholarships.

I didn't apply for a SINGLE scholarship because I was IGNORANT of the possibilities and because I didn't budget any time for scholarships even if I HAD known more about them.

So just by APPLYING for top scholarships, you've probably put yourself in the "1 in 1000" category...

And I really hope this opens your eyes to the VERY REAL possibilities of finishing college apps early and moving on to winning unlimited scholarship money.

After all there is NO LIMIT to the number of scholarships you can apply for, and unlike with your seat at a top college, you can "win" more than one scholarship *at a time* so there is MUCH more benefit to applying for multiple awards.

But- the ONLY way to have TIME for scholarship apps is to already be ahead of the curve on "normal" college apps

Think about it - to WIN all the scholarships other people don't win, you have to APPLY for more scholarships than anyone else you know.

How do you do that? Simple - you start sooner than everyone else and carve out time for extra scholarship apps.

Compared to working a summer job, the hours invested in your scholarships typically pay of from THREE to TEN times better or MORE.

In other words, if you can make $8 an hour bagging groceries over the summer, and you put that time instead into applying for a bunch of scholarships (and hopefully winning a few) - you could see that time on scholarships pay you from $30 to $80 per hour.

There are BILLIONS of dollars in unclaimed scholarships each year that can return $20, $30, $50, even $100 PER HOUR of your time - even if you DON'T win all of them. It only takes a couple to make a HUGE different in your life.

Here's another huge secret - the more scholarships you fill out, the EASIER it gets to fill out even MORE scholarships!

Especially once you've filled out your first couple of scholarship applications, the rest should go MUCH much faster since you can re-use info and answers as well as general essay concepts.

Heck, you might even just recycle large parts of your COLLEGE apps, resume, and activities! You just finished completing all THOSE applications, so you'll have it all fresh in your mind.

By the way, I just gave a HUGE secret that helps explain why just a FEW students end up winning SO MUCH more scholarship money than everyone else!

So if you missed my last point about why scholarship winnings tend to snowball, PLEASE pause, rewind and take notes because it's a really useful secret to understand!

Anyway, winning money for college is something I am REALLY interested in on behalf of my students, so I've actually made an entire online course on **Winning College Scholarships** as well as creative financial aid options for high schoolers.

If you're interested in a comprehensive book on how to find and win THOUSANDS of dollars to pay for college tuition, I want you to go online right now to www.LovetheSAT.com and enroll in my online course on Winning College Scholarships.

That scholarships course is actually one of the biggest courses I've ever made because of how much info I uncovered that I wanted to include.

It doesn't matter if you're a Sophomore, a Senior, or even a seventh-grader.

If you plan to go to college, then you should A) start the process SUPER early and b) apply for about TEN TIMES more scholarships than everyone else.

This might sound like a lot of work - it might sound like it takes a lot of time - and it DOES - but it's an INVESTMENT that pays back a HUNDRED fold as the years of your life go on.

The further you get in your career post-college, the more this stuff will matter to you, since you won't have big student loans, and you'll have graduated with a great degree from a great college and mapped out some of your biggest life goals and dreams.

Honestly, that sounds REALLY inspiring to me and it's what gives me the energy to write an entire book like this one.

I'm INSPIRED by the idea that my students reading this book will THINK AHEAD about their lives, college apps, and scholarships -

And BECAUSE they think ahead, there will be more passion and fulfillment out in the world around me, which ultimately makes the world better for ME and for EVERYONE!

It's like that concept that a butterfly flapping its wings in America can cause a hurricane across the world in China because of chaos effects and feedback loops.

The early start, right now in high school, is the first flap of those wings and it can cause the most incredible results for YOU, years down the line, that pay off in the form of a happy and successful feeling EVERY DAY as you go to do your work for the day.

That's how I feel as an entrepreneur doing what I love. That's how I want you, and everyone I know, to feel.

So, just to review - the process of finding and applying to colleges and scholarships is VERY time consuming - unfortunately, MUCH more than you can possibly imagine, if you've never done it before.

Still, we only go through college and scholarship season ONCE - in our ENTIRE LIVES - and the effort you put in will pay itself back in HUGE ways...

Basically more than ANYTHING else you can do in high school, unless you're already a famous celebrity in high school by some fluke -

In which case, leave a note on the Facebook Wall (www.Facebook.com/LovetheSAT), cause I definitely want to know if any celebrities are taking this class!

Anyway, it is NOT crazy to spend up to 12 to 18 months on your full-time college and scholarship search.

Get out those calendars and create a plan of attack as soon as possible because there's no time to waste.

Again, if you're interested in going much more in-depth on scholarships and financial aid, take a moment now to enroll in my Winning College Scholarships book through the book store or my instructor profile!

One last question that I hope inspires some comments on the Facebook wall:

1. What's your TOP #1 college choice right now, and why EXACTLY is it your favorite option?
2. Do you think you can get in right now?
3. Are your scores, grades and resume strong enough?

Use the Facebook wall (www.Facebook.com/LovetheSAT) to tell me EVERYTHING exciting about your top college pick and why you want to go there, and I'll see you in the next chapter.

Further Reading:
www.LovetheSAT.com/how-to-get-in-to-college-the-complete-guide

22. ATHLETICS, EXTRACURRICULARS AND LEADERSHIP POSITIONS

So, what do YOU do OUTSIDE of high school?

Unless you're planning to "risk it all" on some specific talent like athletics or performing arts AND you're making signficant progress already towards those goals, for most of us, school should always be the number-one priority.

That being said, it's a cliche that "Variety is the spice of life" and most of us WANT and NEED more than just ONE major focus in our lives.

On the OTHER hand, there's that OTHER cliche: "Jack of all trades, master of none" - meaning, if you try to do TOO many things, there's simply no WAY to get incredibly good at any ONE of them.

It's a spectrum - or a balance - or a seesaw. Depends on how you want to look at it.

But because of this natural spectrum, I think that when it comes to sports and activities OUTSIDE of your MAIN focus (which is usually either high school, college, or your career), then one to three additional hobbies, sports, groups, or activities is the sweet spot.

Now I'm not trying to convince you to live life my way, I'm just saying -

Everyone has the same 24 hours in a day and if YOU want to be good at something, chances are that many OTHER people also want to be "good" at it -

Leading to an arms race where the general talent pool just keeps getting better and better; which means you need to SPECIALIZE more in order to stand out.

That very specialization NATURALLY means less time for OTHER things that you want to be good at.

Deep down we all know this, but there's an important consequence as well:

You have to KNOW what your priorities are outside of school, and LITERALLY be able to rank them in a top 1-5 list or whatever number of priorities you have.

And THIS goes back to some of the central lessons I've been trying to teach throughout this book:

You have to IDENTIFY and KNOW the personal priorities that TRULY matter to you (even if other people don't fully agree with them).

Because when the INEVITABLE scheduling conflicts and energy limitations come up, you don't waste time debating.

You just KNOW that you should go with the higher priority commitment.

Now, high school is a time to try new things out, for sure.

I mean, the truth is you haven't even been ALIVE long enough to try everything there is in the world, BUT make no mistake:

Somehow or another, many kids in high school ARE already figuring out, or even already KNOW "who they are" and what they want to DO with their lives, and they are already focusing ALL their efforts around succeeding in that area of life.

Again, I've noticed that these kids do what they feel they MUST do, EVEN if others around them don't fully agree or support it.

It's that TRUE passion of "I have to do this, this matters to ME" that drives these kids towards success EVEN STARTING IN HIGH SCHOOL, which I think is one of the best models to copy if you can do it.

As much as possible, that's what I recommend - the sooner you IDENTIFY the things you really LOVE to do, the more time you can spend getting good at it.

So pause your reading in a moment and spend the time to make a list of the following:

First, list your current activities and sports.

Next, create some sort of personalize number-based RANKING of all your current activities and sports.

The more analysis you do in this stage, the better - which activities require the most time commitment and energy?

Are those the SAME activities that you find the most enjoyable and personally rewarding?

Which activities seem the best for your long-term future?

Asking yourself these questions, and TRYING your best to assign some kind of rankings to your answers, will help you make wise long-term decisions on what to keep and what to drop.

Step three, brainstorm activities and sports you'd REALLY like to try at least once in your life.

This can be anything from the ordinary to the exotic, and in fact I HOPE your list includes a big mix of the entire spectrum!

For example, I have a list that's almost a hundred items long:

It includes goals from "stay reasonably physically healthy throughout my life" to "go skydiving at least 5 times" to "Motorcycle to the farthest-south point of South America" to "write and record an album of original music."

What they all have in common is they INSPIRE me and get me pumped-up to work hard and use my time efficiently.

That's what I think YOU want in YOUR list as well.

The final step once you have your list ready is to make an action plan -

And this isn't too hard.

You kind of just have to trust your gut and look at what your ranking system and numbers are trying to tell you.

Maybe you should DROP the lowest-ranked activities from your list.

Or, does your current activities list look awfully empty, in which case maybe it's time to try out a couple of activities from your wishlist this semester?

The goal of setting aside 15 minutes to do this exercise is twofold:

One, to find NEW stuff that you really love to do, and TWO, to cut back wasted effort on things you've already tried that you don't really love to do.

Here's a pro tip about scheduling -

You MAY be doing something, some activity or sport or something, during your weeks specifically because you think you HAVE to or because you think someone ELSE'S opinion of you DEPENDS on doing this thing...

... But deep down it's something you really DON'T enjoy or dread going to, and no matter how you look at this thing it's just NEVER gonna be something you really care for.

You need to be really TOUGH with yourself in these situations - and I know because I've been there many times before, and sometimes I WASTED too much time before I left...

But we are all able to fall victim to the TRAP of pursuing someone else's dream or trying to impress our peers or whatever it is that takes us off the path of what we REALLY care more about.

This is especially true in high school where peer pressure is intense, parents seem to control your every move, the media and advertising is trying to buy your soul, AND you've barely had a chance to try anything for yourself yet and see what you really like to do!

That's why I am saying so strongly that if you DON'T like doing something that you're doing in high school you should STOP - IMMEDIATELY - and ask if you're doing it to please or impress someone else.

And if so I highly recommend cutting it out of your schedule so you have the time to find NEW things that you might like more because the sooner you KNOW about the good stuff in life that makes you REALLY happy, the better.

Now I'm not trying to offend anyone! and you should ALWAYS ask what the value is:

For example, I hated running laps in high school, BUT it's true that fitness is important, and without sports and a P.E. coach, honestly I might have been too lazy to do any real exercise on my own and gotten really unhealthy before I wised up enough to take care of my body -

So i'm GLAD I didn't cut sports out of my high school schedule back in the day, even though honestly I didn't really love them so much.

So you have to think critically, you have to think long-term, and you have to think like an adult.

But, if you can't justify WHY you're doing an activity or sport and you don't even LIKE the time you spend on it, then I think I'm giving pretty solid advice to say CUT IT OUT of your schedule as soon as you possibly can.

When it comes to earning Leadership positions, everything I'm saying in this lesson goes double or even triple.

Because one thing you will NOT probably enjoy very much is if you somehow force yourself to end up in a position of leadership for a sport or activity that you don't really love.

Probably in this situation you will sabotoge yourself by not really giving your full effort or just generally not wanting to be there which is a REALLY bad thing for a leader's mindset and will end in disaster and a lot of wasted time and energy and disappointment.

Besides, the key to EASILY winning coveted and competitive leadership positions is to LOVE the sport or activity you are involved in.

Leadership positions are just like an INTENSIFICATION of the previous level.

These positions aren't PERKS, they are... INEVITABILITIES.

Ultimately, in the LONG run, the people who care the most and work the hardest in their field will tend to rise to the top.

Everything else is just temporary, lucky, or fraudulent.

If you look at the friends and peers you admire who are in positions of leadership, ask yourself one question:

Do they seem to LIKE what they're doing?

I bet you anything, at least four out of five of them are REALLY into whatever they're leading - be it a rock band or a robotics club or a cheer team.

To share a brief but hopefully enlightening bit from my own life:

In high school I really struggled to find significant leadership positions.

I liked lacrosse, but I wasn't committed enough to sports to earn my place as a captain.

I liked music, but I didn't have enough initiative yet to organize and lead my own groups.

I didn't really care about student government, so I experienced a massive and humiliating failure when I ran for that, because I *didn't even care in the first place* if I got elected.

Then, when I got to college, I started to really discover my love for music by being more active with my piano practice and broadening what I listened to.

Interestingly enough, by sophomore year I had organized and led my first chamber-music group which was INCREDIBLY fun, like one of the best things I've EVER done.

(For those of you who are unfamiliar with the term, "chamber music" usually refers to a small group of classical musicians, typically around three to five of them in a small room together)

I played piano, and I would find string players like violinists and cellists, and I would pick the music, find us a faculty coach, and organize and schedule rehearsals and performances.

This was an ENORMOUS amount of work, I mean truly spectacular, to try and have to keep this going WHILE in the middle of college, because this was just one small facet of what I was doing.

But, it didn't feel like an OBLIGATION, it felt like the BEST part of my week -

And my point is that once I engaged my PASSIONS and INTERESTS, it was easy to power-up and find leadership positions NATURALLY that I also EXCELLED in because I really cared about the field I was in.

And guess what? I also had much more natural motivation to organize my time better, because my OWN clutter and inefficiencies and procrastination would just hold ME back on the goals /wanted!

So I naturally learned to cut through the garbage and fight for time for the stuff I really wanted to do.

And, since graduating college I feel like I've even taken it to the NEXT level.

By discovering my passion for entrepreneurship, I've realized how INCREDIBLY hard-working I can be when I'm working for mySELF towards goals I believe in.

So, from FAILING HORRIBLY in my attempts to win student government leadership, I've actually ended up starting and running my own company and feeling a daily sense of TOTAL INDEPENDENCE and PASSION.

It's actually pretty funny to look back on.

You know, they say "Comedy is just tragedy plus time!"

That's kind of how I feel looking back on my very youthful attempts to win leadership positions in fields, clubs or activities I didn't really care about in the first place - just to try and impress people around me, I suppose.

Your EXACT goals might be slightly different than mine but I'm willing to BET that **if you're living an independent, passionate life you will be a LONG way towards being happy and successful on a level that many people will never touch.**

It took me a LONG time to put these pieces together - about 26 years - and really get working on things I love.

So I'm hoping that as a student of this book you're going to COMPLETELY surpass me and discover and follow your passions years and years earlier than I have.

Not that I really have any regrets - looking back, I think I can see how I needed to take each step one after another to get to where I am today.

So you see, when you love what you're working on, it never really feels like work and you'll naturally want to do it more and get better at it more rapidly than people who AREN'T really interested on a personal level.

In the end you'll have fun, get good at something you love, and inspire and lead the people around you.

Now I want you to listen again to what I just said:

If you follow this gameplan you will have FUN, get GOOD at something you love to do, and you will inspire and lead your friends and family around you...

... and THAT -

- To me, THAT is basically the definintion of being happy and successful, and THAT is EXACTLY the end goal of good time management.

You can start now in High School by dropping activities you DON'T enjoy and filling your schedule with just a few hand-picked, life-enriching pastimes that define and fit YOU to a Tee.

Now tell me - what do YOU love to do most outside of school?

Leave a quick message on the Facebook page (www.Facebook.com/LovetheSAT) and let me know your favorite activity, sport, club, or team that you do outside of high school and what it is that makes you LOVE doing it every single time.

It's so cool to be inspired by hearing what everyone in this class loves to do! So, please take just a moment to share your favorite pastime and what you LOVE about it, and I'll see you in the next chapter!

Additional Reading:
www.eSATPrepTips.com/college-application-resume-activities

23. MAINTAINING A SOCIAL LIFE: PEER PRESSURE AND TIME MANAGEMENT

I've worked with hundreds of high school students one-on-one and in group lessons, but more importantly, I was once a teenager and high schooler MYSELF.

So, I'm speaking fairly confidently when I say that for many high schoolers, SOCIAL LIFE and your friend group is probably the single most interesting and important thing to you on a daily basis.

In this chapter I want us to spend some time thinking about your social life and how it affects your ability to manage your time and get things done.

Now, first things first. Social life IS important and I'm not going to tell you otherwise.

It might seems like your parents and teachers are always trying to suck up all your time with homework and activities so that you never actually have any TIME to hang out with your friends.

Or, whenever you finally get a chance to relax with your friends or do something fun, it seems like your parents are always blowing the whistle too soon and calling you back home to study for your finals, or whatever.

But, that doesn't mean your parents and teachers don't WANT you to have a social life.

What I've usually found is that none of the adults in your life are FULLY aware of just HOW MUCH work you have to do, so they always think it's ok to give "just one more assignment" or "one more chore" or whatever -

Not realizing how much you would kill to just get some time with your friends, free from rules and obligations.

Other than being a time to get some relief from all your work, social time is also

incredibly important for the skills and charisma we develop through interacting with our peers and friends.

Without a doubt, social skills are important in college, the workplace and in adult life, so now's the ideal time to start working on them.

It might seem a little over-dramatic to say that hanging out with your friends is important because it makes you a better adult, but whatever, it's totally true!

And right now in this book about time management, I'm thinking of all the reasons that social life is an important and worthy use of your time.

But, I'm also thinking about the HUGE risks that can come up during social time during classes, after school, and on the weekends:

And please don't roll your eyes too hard, but I'm talking about things like peer pressure, getting into trouble, drug and alcohol use, cutting classes etc -

It's nothing personal, it's just something teenagers have ALWAYS done; it's only human to look for ways to rebel and have new experiences, especially when certain things are "off limits" or "against the rules" -

And in a group with your friends, it can be easy to lose sight of the boundaries and egg each other on to break the rules perhaps a little too much.

It's one of those things where it's all fun and games until SUDDENLY you've crossed a line and you realize you might be in serious trouble.

For example, everyone eventually learns that if they SPEED on public roads, they'll see cop lights flashing in their rear view mirror from time to time.

So, if you take RISKS and test your luck, you will sometimes come up on the BAD side of luck and then there will be consequences that you can't necessarily undo.

So, in terms of time management, I just needed to take a moment in this chapter to remind you to make SMART decisions.

Or maybe more importantly, try not to make any really DUMB decisions that could get you in trouble because those are the things that WILL catch up to you eventually.

Nothing will set you back SO MUCH as getting in big trouble during high school.

This kind of stuff can jeopardize your entire college and career experience, believe it or not, because although MOST mistakes you make in high school will be completely forgotten with time, the truth is a BIG mistake in high school can ABSOLUTELY haunt you for the rest of your life.

Even an accumulation of SMALL mistakes in high school can hold you back since your college and first job options won't be quite as good as they would have been.

Look, I don't mean to be scary - it's only because I care so much about your success that I'm emphasizing this section so strongly.

It's when we're with our friends that we're MOST likely to compromise on "who we are" and let go of our own personal values, even temporarily, in order to fit in with the crowd.

I'm suggesting that when it comes to living your life and managing your time, it's incredibly important to keep a short leash on this natural tendency.

You HAVE to watch yourself and keep yourself from EVER spiraling out of control due to peer pressure, because it only takes ONE time for things to go really wrong and then ALL your hard work so far can go to waste.

On a similar subject, many high schoolers will say studying is not "cool". So, you may not want to really brag about it with your friends, unless they're really smart and studious like you.

My reccomendation is that if your peer group REALLY hates studying - (well first of all maybe you should find a new group of friends!) - but, if they really hate school, just dont TELL them about your hard work..

And dont CALL ATTENTION to your newfound good grades, passions in life, time-management and study skills.

Most of us are pretty focused on ourselves, so if you never call attention to your success, probably your friends will never really notice or care too much how well you're doing in your classes, and you can go on BEING FRIENDS with them but ALSO excelling in school, goal-setting and time management.

And now one final thought - always keep in mind that quote, "time you enjoy wasting is not time wasted," which means if you're really having a good time, then it can't be THAT big a waste of time, right?

I think it's partially true, and we should always remember to enjoy ourselves and not take life TOO seriously, but you also have to contend with reality someday -

Like the need to graduate from high school, get into a good college, and make enough money to live and accomplish your life's work so that you feel happy and satisfied with your life on every level.

So, ever feel like you've made a bad decision due to peer pressure?

I know I have. It's ok, we've all been there. Get it off your chest and share it on the Facebook wall (www.Facebook.com/LovetheSAT) so we can all share a good laugh about it and relieve some pent-up old anxieties.

If we all share our dumb mistakes due to social pressure, I bet we'll see that EVERYONE is susceptible to peer pressure from time to time.

Head to the Facebook wall (www.Facebook.com/LovetheSAT) and share your story, and I'll see you in the next chapter!

24. STUDY GROUPS: DO THEY REALLY HELP?

In this chapter we'll cover the topic of study groups in high school and have an honest discussion about how helpful they really are in terms of saving you time and getting you better results and grades in school.

For the purposes of this discussion, when I say "study group" I just mean any group of TWO or more students who have arranged to meet, ON THEIR OWN, for the stated purpose of studying or working on a specific class that they all share.

It could be two friends working on separate art-class projects in the same garage, or it could be a self-arranged group of 15 top students who routinely meet to study for AP chemistry on Friday nights, it doesn't really matter.

Similar principles, potential benefits, and risks will generally apply to all group-study dynamics and it's important to make use of study groups with open eyes and personal reflection.

When it comes to effective study group use, make sure you follow the key time management rule, "KNOW YOURSELF," and your personality and style.

Getting into a good study group can actually be much trickier than it seems, because the same type of study group is NOT right for all students.

So always remember one of the most important rules of time management - KNOW yourself.

Do you do better on your own? With one or two friends? In a small group? In a big group?

Can you ORGANIZE and LEAD a group? Or will you depend on your classmates?

In this case, you also have to KNOW YOUR FRIENDS - because it's not about who you LIKE the best, it's about who ADDS the most to the study group.

Now, not all subjects are created equal when it comes to study groups.

Some of the best classes and topics for study groups are the type where reviewing notes together can help the group identify key points from the teacher, the readings, and class themes.

In more science- or math-based books, try writing practice problems for each other to complete.

If you REALLY want to learn a subject, it's incredibly helpful to create problems yourself, like a teacher would.

This is something I know personally, because I've been a tutor for so long.

Flashcards also work well in small groups.

Hardworking friends can help keep each other company while you MAKE flashcards, and even STUDY them together.

Actually, working with a friend can add a strong EMOTIONAL connection to your memories and actually HELP YOU REMEMBER flashcards more easily... but ONLY if you both actually buckle down and STUDY HARD together.

It won't just work because you're sitting in the same room laughing at a story about your school day. You have to actually work hard and study.

It can also be really fun to do freeform, creative projects that aren't for school - like making art or music or movies with your friends, or even starting a business together.

Now, I think some of the WORST classes and topics for study groups are ones that involve intensive memorization or drilling flashcards - that's something you just need to do on your own.

This also goes for performance art like memorizing music or lines for a high school play - not always so good for working in a group.

On the other hand, smart drama students could organize mock rehearsals together in order to get more comfortable with each other's lines before a performance!

Another time that group work is not a great idea, is for independent essays or research projects.

Actually, anything where INDEPENDENT work is expected doesn't work so well in a group, since you don't want to influence each other - which COULD be seen as plagiarism or bending the rules of the assignement.

However, it CAN be nice to work in the same ROOM on projects because it creates a "productive feeling" - but I do recommend you bring headphones to create some private space.

One of the most important points I'm trying to convey is that the BEST students never try to make study groups into more than they are.

They can't solve your study or homework problems for you.

Now, what's the BEST-case scenario for a good study group?

IF everyone participates and contributes - you get what author Napoleon Hill called the "mastermind effect" where you all MULTIPLY each other's thoughts.

And that is EXTREMELY powerful, but it's also a little RARE in high school because not everyone is so committed to their grades and classes.

Basically, a helpful study group comes from the PEOPLE who participate in it.

If everyone in the study group operating on a high level in the class, INCLUDING YOURSELF, then the group will most likely be successful and produce some of the top students in the room.

You know that feeling where you're having a really intense conversation with your best friend about some subject that you both care deeply about, and you can almost start reading their mind and finishing each other's sentences?

That's the idea behind the Mastermind, but it requires PASSION and INTELLIGENCE from ALL its participants or it usually will just fizzle out.

(One a side note, if you want to know more about the Mastermind Principle, go read the book Think and Grow Rich by Napoleon Hill.

I actually used one of his quotes early in the book, and he's one of the BEST all-time researchers and authors of how to be more productive and successful - that book is one of my favorites)

I would argue that the CENTRAL PURPOSE of any study group should be to cause this "Mastermind Effect" to take place..

Otherwise you are guaranteed to be more efficient just STUDYING ON YOUR OWN, because that "study group" is just going to fizzle out into "social hour."

I think that's one of the main reasons study groups can actually HURT you quite a bit -

It's because they often serve as COVER for what is REALLY just extra *social* time.

Why it's really DANGEROUS is that you're sitting with your friends there TELLING each other it's a "study group."

So you'll probably subconsciously count the time towards "homework time" on your calendar, and because you attended the "study group" you'll probably feel more lazy or complacent about the upcoming test or quiz.

In this sort of scenario it's easy to see how a so-called study group would be a waste of time at best.

Study groups are ALL vulnerable to disruptive members.

The principle that a chain is only as strong as its weakest link DEFINITELY tends to apply to study groups.

What's worse, without a leader the group is often aimless or unproductive.

Furthermore, the self-appointed "leader" is NOT the same as the person who knows the MOST about the subject - that person might be much quieter, and then get spoken over by louder students!

Or, for, example, you might invite your BEST FRIEND to study with you but the truth is, they're just NOT a "grade-A student," even as much as you love them as a friend.

Meanwhile, the top student in your class might be a little bit obnoxious, so you choose not to ask them to the study group.

I guess what I mean is, and I'm not judging this because it's totally normal, but in high school a lot of times "study group" is just a cover up for "I'm going to go hang out with my friends."

I did it too, but that doesn't change the fact that these were among my LEAST-productive meetings in school, so let's agree to try and minimize these.

All I'm really saying is, if you're going to go hang out with friends, GO hang out with friends - just don't tell people it's a STUDY GROUP, and especially don't tell YOURSELF that!

So, you know I love sharing a little bit from my own life so here's what study groups were like for ME, a fairly serious student but still just your normal high schooler who liked to goof around.

If I'm being completely honest, almost ALL of my study groups in high school were nearly wastes of time, because it was just so RARE that the WHOLE group was really there to buckle down and study.

Practically always there was someone WASTING the group's time and distracting everybody or slowing everyone down - and sometimes it was ME.

In the classes I LIKED in high school I was usually in the top 10% of the class so, not to trying sound arrogant but I didn't think I would gain much from study groups since I already felt solid on the material.

Then on the FLIP side, In the classes I actually STRUGGLED with in high school like chemistry or my hardest math classes, I didn't have good enough notes or class participation to actually gain much from the study group, so I was basically the kid you DON'T want in the study group!

Now, it could entirely be ME and that I just was bad luck or something, but looking back, I just dont know if most of us are ready for serious, high-pressure study groups in high school!

/certainly wasn't! I think that's part of the reason I lean towards PERSONAL time management for your high school studies rather than attempting to do everything by committee.

On the other hand, it IS really important to learn to be an effective contributor to a group - since teamwork is such a big part of life and career.

So maybe it's just the EFFORT of trying to form a good study group in high school that's the most important thing.

Does that make any sense? Sometimes we just need to learn to TRY to form a good study group in high school, even if it's nearly impossible to actually SUCCEED?

Well luckily, in college the average quality of student INCREASED, and so did my work ethic and my interest in my chosen subjects.

For example, the chamber music groups that I led were actually a lot like study groups -

They had similar characteristics of setting goals, organizing classmates, leading practices or study sessions, aiming towards a final performance and then doing it all again!

Then again, I also found that the majority of my work in college was project-based, such as researching and writing essays, or composing music, or practicing piano -

And that stuff was VERY personal and couldn't be shared or divided up with my classmates.

I did find out that some study groups in college WERE good for TESTS and FINALS- especially for IDENTIFYING what we needed to study - **and if your professor is hosting a review, GO, GO, GO.**

Make sure you attend ALL instructor-led review sessions!

The VERY-information heavy books (like foreign languages and hard sciences) are some of the best classes for professor-led reviews because the DIFFICULTY of the material is just very tough for beginners and even intermediate-level students.

So the professors tend to know MUCH more than the students do.

Something like a literature book, while equally respectable as a language or science book, is probably EASIER to study on your OWN -

Because we all are probably pretty good readers already if we're in a college-level literature book by choice, and our teacher won't be SO incredibly far ahead of us in the basic reading skills and knowledge they way they probably are in science, and higher-level math or foreign language books.

Not only are professor-run sessions generally MUCH more useful than any student-run study session, you'll also sometimes be NOTICED by the professor and that will sometimes help with partial credit when they are grading your test.

Be sure the professor or teaching assistant hosting the review session KNOWS you are there - take a moment to introduce yourself and ask a smart question to them 1-on-1 if you can!

This can actually affect your grade in key moments when the professor gives you a little extra credit for putting forth the time and effort to attend the study session and stand out.

Try it, I promise it will help. It's pretty much how I got through Organic Chemistry as a sophomore in college.

If the professor won't be there, it can still be valuable to attend student-organized review sessions - as long as you've stayed at least somewhat engaged in class.

Luckily, the AVERAGE level of student commitment is much, MUCH higher than the average in high school, so you should find it significantly easier to convince good students to join your study group.

There's so much going on in a lot of college classes, that many times even the best students won't catch everything important.

So, there's a lot of value to convincing other classmates to work as a team, even if they're a little stronger or weaker in class than you are.

By comparing notes and ID'ing the TOP info together, you can work together to create a study sheet that you THEN each go use on your own.

You can use the group cheat sheet to make personal flash cards for the words and formulas, and break it down on your OWN as you memorize what the group identified as most important.

But always be aware that other students can't MEMORIZE for you, so just because you're in the ROOM with someone who's really on top of their college class, doesn't mean that YOU will just naturally absorb their wisdom by being near them.

You have to STUDY the info like they did. Ultimately it all comes down to you.

Now, as we wind this discussion down, here are what I hope will be some useful tips on how to control this risks to maximize the rewards of your OWN study groups in high school and college.

First of all, be the organizer or leader of the study group.

Try to know the most about the subject!

And, like any study or homework situation, your environment matters. Pick a good, quiet spot with comfortable places to sit and work.

PLAN the meeting and decide the group goals ahead of time, or at least set some guidelines for the group.

Don't tolerate distractions and don't let disruptive students stay in the group.

And, "casually" let the teacher know you're leading and organizing the group -

In fact, ask if the teacher or professor could schedule some time to MEET with the group!

On the balance, the BEST study groups are typically smaller, tightly-knit groups of top students who share notes and identify key class information for mutual benefit....

Thus, achieving a "mastermind" effect that is smarter in a group than any of the individuals are on their own.

The WORST study groups are time-wasters typically dragged down by a lack of organization and leadership OR one or two "weak links" who break the chain of the mastermind group.

In my experience the most common mistake is having a social hour but calling it a study group.

Overall, I PERSONALLY get mixed results from study groups; overall they did not perform very well in High School, and only got me average results in college compared to studying hard on my own.

However as I've matured and gotten into my career, I've also come to appreciate that many big problems cannot be solved individually.

To TRULY make a dent in the universe these days, it seems you have to know either how to LEAD a team, or how to be PART of one.

And better yet, you should learn to do both.

But, there's no real point to being a member of a BAD study group...

So, if you're dedicated to the idea of having a study group, I believe achieving the "mastermind effect" should be the only goal - so pick carefully who you study with.

If the teacher or professor ever hosts a study session outside of class, GO TO IT.

The bottom line is, never be afraid to test the waters, but plan to be a leader and always strive to maintain the highest standards for your study group.

Now, leave me a quick note on the Facebook wall: (www.Facebook.com/LovetheSAT)

1. What's YOUR experience with study groups like?
2. Do you think they're effective or ineffective for you, and how come?

Take a moment to pause and leave your thoughts before going on to the next chapter!

25. WHAT TO DO WITH YOUR WEEKENDS IN HIGH SCHOOL

The use of your weekends in high school - what you do, who you see, and how you schedule yourself - is one of those MAJOR things that separates high-honor roll students from everyone else.

You don't have to give up on having fun - as with most things, the key is balance, planning and prioritization.

You see, each weekend is really like a little "mini-vacation" - circling around once per week to give you some CHOICE in how you spend your time.

In fact, you should refer to the "vacation planning" chapter in this book to get the connection between how you spend your weekends and how you spend your vacations...

... Because what weekends and vacations have in common is that while some people use their vacations to laze around, others find a way to enjoy themselves AND get stuff done.

Actually PLANNING your weekends in advance is simple, yet it's one of the most important ways of getting more out of your Saturday and Sunday.

The trick is to always use Friday after school to plan your weekend; or better yet, use the end of each Sunday to plan the coming weekend in advance.

And, as with everything we've discussed in the book KEEP A JOURNAL - possibly a specific "Weekend Journal" section.

Try and particularly notice how you spend your weekends and what you can improve upon.

Remember that the purpose is to get stuff done AND get time to relax and have fun. SO, don't just record what you get DONE, also record what you do for FUN.

Over time, the purpose of this weekend journalling is to experience a sense of insight and power over your weekends that helps you feel happy and fulfilled in life.

High school is also a great time to do this since school days are so rigorously scheduled but weekends are generally so unstructured.

Think of your weekends, and what you choose to do with them, as PRACTICE for the free-flowing time management you'll experience when you're out of school and in the "real life" working world.

Now, one of the top priorities of any high school weekend, is to CATCH UP ON SLEEP, but don't overdo it. Too MUCH sleep can be as bad as not ENOUGH sleep.

The real secret of having energy on the weekends is to have a sense of PURPOSE - what did you plan to DO with your weekend? What are you going to ACCOMPLISH or ENJOY on Saturday and Sunday?

When you are EXCITED about the weekend, you won't want to spend the whole morning sleeping!

Unfortunately, the weekends in high school aren't ALL about sleep, enjoyment, and life purpose - we also have to get our weekend homework and studying done before Monday rolls around again.

How do you prioritize, and when do you do your schoolwork on the weekends?

Well, like everything else, starting early is key. For example, if you start your assignments midday on Saturday, instead of waiting till Sunday after dinner, you'll carry less stress over the entire weekend.

Or, if you start homework Sunday MORNING instead of Sunday NIGHT, you will lower the risk of a panic situation.

So, how do YOU handle things right now? Do you do your weekend homework in the mornings?

Or, do you wait till the afternoon or evening?

Here's another place where journaling will help - take note of when you are at your BEST and WORST energy levels on Saturday and Sunday and use this information to plan your coming weekends.

Then, you should try to get your hardest assignments done when your energy on the weekend is typically HIGHEST.

If you're planning your weekends in advance, doing your weekend assignments as early as you can, and maximizing your "high energy" points, you'll find that you get a LOT more done on your weekends WITHOUT needing to sacrifice much time relaxing, sleeping, or hanging our with your friends.

Here's another big secret - 99% of high schoolers sleep late on weekend mornings.

SO on Saturday morning - most of your friends will probably be asleep, nothing entertaining is really going on, and it's the PERFECT time to do your hardest weekend schoolwork and get it over with.

Then when all the fun starts in the AFTERNOONS and EVENINGS of the weekend, you can go have fun with less work hanging over your head!

Don't forget that weekends are PRIME time for SAT and ACT test prep like practice tests and homework sections, and weekends are also IDEAL for long sessions of sit-down free reading to improve your speed, comprehension, and vocabulary.

Or, they're one of the ONLY times you can get ahead on college and scholarship research and applications.

For example, you could use the time on weekend mornings to start my Winning College Scholarships course (visit www.LovetheSAT.com to get it) and take small steps weekend by weekend.

While your friends are sleeping in, you'll be earning THOUSANDS of dollars in college money that you WON'T have to pay back later - meaning, when you're done with college, you'll be WAY ahead in life.

That might mean a nicer living situation, more choices in life, the ability to travel or buy a car after college, or WHATEVER it means to you to save some money.

What's it worth to YOU? **Are you ready** to lose a little sleep on Saturday morning in order to live an exciting and rich life? I know I am.

Also, if you're taking part in sports or activities or extracurriculars in high school you'll also find that **these teams and clubs eat up a LOT of your time on the weekends with mandatory activities like practices, games, meetings, and performances.**

It's up to YOU to ANTICIPATE how draining this can be of your time and energy, and also your job to predict the SOCIAL element that eats up time before and after.

For example, if on Friday after school you're supposed to go early to the game for warm-up and stretching, and then stay late as the team goes out for pizza....

That's going to cut into your weekend homework and relaxing time as WELL as cost you a lot of energy and focus after a long week.

Basically, you should budget DOUBLE time - twice as much as you think you'll need - for these weekend sports and activities so you have time to socialize and RECOVER your energy from participating.

Then, at worst, you'll have a little extra time to pad your schedule with and at best you'll have prevented a panic situation or school-grade disaster.

On particularly busy weekends when you are tied to teams, groups, and other people's schedules, DONT try to pack too much in on your own time - instead, reduce your to-do list and focus on choosing your priorities wisely.

This same rule also applies to your weekend SOCIAL life.

Sure, weekends are great - and you should enjoy them with friends.

BUT - you also need SLEEP - because one really late night on the weekend can mess up your whole upcoming week of school and activities.

And DONT do anything stupid on the weekends, or at least dont get CAUGHT doing anything stupid!

I know that teenagers use alcohol and drugs sometimes, but these things slow you down, harm your health and can lead to SERIOUS trouble that invalidates all the hard work you've put in.

I won't start sermonizing, because my point is that you need to have fun with your friends - but please do it in a smart way that doesn't harm your health or steal all your energy for the upcoming busy week.

Finally, there's the need for some downtime - whether you realize it or not.

I'm not talking about SOCIAL downtime - that takes energy! And I'm not talking about SLEEPING downtime either.

The downtime I'm talking about is mid-level brain engagement like free reading, taking a long walk, listening to music, watching HIGH-QUALITY shows or documentaries, playing board games, and all sorts of other mellow activities like that.

You might be learning an instrument for fun or practicing your cooking skills.

It's NOT something to do with school, it's NOT "just sitting around," and it's NOT an obligation you have for something else.

For me, reading, motorcycling, and playing guitar and piano all fill this need for an enjoyable activity that's not too high-pressure but also not lazy.

I want you to PAUSE now and brainstorm your own ideas for a list of downtime activities that fit YOU.

Here are the takeaways for this lesson:

Weekends are one of the best times in high school, because they're like a recurring "mini holiday" that comes around every week.

Your top priorities for each weekend should be to recover, sleep, get homework done, and get some personal time.

Get your homework and studying done as SOON as possible - particularly when your friends are still sleeping, so that you can have fun with them later without any guilt or stress.

Work on your test prep on Saturday or Sunday since it's tough to set aside time during the week.

Or, use that time for college and scholarship applications.

It's also good to take part in sports and activities that add some additional activities and structure to your weekend.

But, be careful of the enormous time and energy commitment that these activities often require. Don't overcommit to stuffing your calendar.

Hang out with your friends in afternoon or evening after you've already been productive.

Be smart and safe - don't get into trouble... and don't stay up till three in the morning on Saturday, because it will take a WEEK to catch up on the sleep and you can't afford to be groggy for a whole week.

Finally, use your free time for something more worthwhile than just watching TV. Use the weekends to work on your favorite hobbies and interests OUTSIDE of schoolwork.

Think of weekends as a mini-college preview, since they give a taste of scheduling freedom - especially compared to the fixed schedule of your school days Monday through Friday.

So, what do YOU currently do with your weekends?

Is there some reason for you to jump out of bed on Saturday and Sunday?

Or, do you feel like you SLEEP all weekend long - and maybe it feels like you NEED it?

I'm REALLY curious and psyched up to hear how you spend the average weekend AND what you think your "ideal" normal weekend would look like.

For most of us, weekends are one of the best things in school and in life. I think it's really fun to talk about them :)

Take some time to PAUSE and describe your CURRENT weekend and your PERFECT weekend on the Facebook wall **(www.Facebook.com/LovetheSAT)**, and I'll see you in the next chapter!

26. MAKING THE MOST OF YOUR BREAKS AND VACATIONS IN HIGH SCHOOL

In this chapter let's talk about your high school breaks and holidays and how they relate to overall goals and time management.

As we tried to define it in the beginning, time management is about effective use of your limited time, leading to more personal fulfillment.

Holidays test this to the max because the general mood is "dont do anything" BUT it's a paradox because these are EXTREMELY rare opportunities for students to have huge amounts of open free time in their days.

In fact, adults experience this as well - it's one of the reasons that, surprisingly, a large percentage of adults have a somewhat NEGATIVE experience of the holidays - which are supposed to be run and relaxing!

My theory is, one reason is that a lot of people just act like SLOTHS during their holidays and actually get FARTHER from their TRUE hopes and dreams.

This causes them to feel frustrated or to realize that they feel something "off" but can't pinpoint it.

The point is, holidays give a lot of sudden FREE TIME which can lead to some unexpected results that aren't always positive.

I think you need to plan WAY in advance how you will use your "vacation time" to both recharge your batteries AND get important work done at key moments during each year of high school.

So, let's try to hit the highlights of breaks and vacations, particularly during Junior and Senior year of high school.

First of all, here are some of the major key tasks that work really well around your breaks and vacations - please take a few notes:

- College research, college visits, college applications, and college essays.
- SAT and ACT prep and practice testing.
- Studying for tests and school finals and finishing end-of-term projects
- Doing long reading assignments and extra free reading time.
- Taking other online courses with Love the SAT! to prep for specific classes or supplemental personal goals.
- Making and memorizing vocab flashcards
- Doing additional tutoring in your weakest subjects.
- Working on fine arts projects like learning a piece of music, memorizing a script, taking pictures for your photography portfolio, or any other projects you care about.
- Getting a bunch of exercise and outdoor time and sleep to help your health.
- Unwinding, catching a quick break, or my favorite...
- And, seeing or doing something new to refresh your energy in life.

Let's cover each of the major yearly breaks and explore some smart ways you can use them.

First of all, SUMMER.

Summer break is obviously the most famous of all high school breaks - nearly 3 months of seemingly wide-open time to sit around doing nothing!

The only thing is... it never turns out that way. If you sit around all summer, you'll get bored to TEARS in just a few weeks.

Actually, many high schoolers find their summers just as crazy-busy as their school years.

With off-season sports, summer camps, family vacations, time with friends, and summer reading assignments it can seem like there's no free time at all!

My advice for summer is this: make the most of every summer and keep trying new things.

For example, try having a paid job one year, and go to summer camp another year.

But, ALWAYS use summer to prep your schoolwork, enhance your resume, get higher SAT/ACT scores and complete your college and scholarship applications.

Keep progress moving forward on the end goal of finding and getting accepted to a great college.

Summer is NOT the ideal time for campus visits since colleges aren't in session, so instead, work on your resume and activities.

Your summer resume can actually matter a LOT to your college acceptance odds.

Seniors and Juniors especially MUST make strategic decisions with their summer activities and commitments.

What will help you get into college? Do LOTS of that stuff over summer.

This also helps prevent "the Summer effect" of getting super-rusty and lazy in school and work.

The weird thing about being super-lazy over summer is that it's not even fun!

Maybe if you're sitting around getting bored and rusty this summer, try signing up for one of my online courses for college-bound teens at www.LovetheSAT.com to keep you moving forward, because a long summer vacation is one the absolute best times to study with me on the side.

Basically, active and productive summers will ALWAYS be more fun and rewarding than lazy, passive summers.

So, plan in advance what you'll do with yours this year!

Spring Break is one of the next-most popular breaks and offers from 1-2 weeks of vacation time when you need it most - right near the end of the school year.

Honestly, if you need to use this time for a REAL vacation I wouldn't blame you.

My dad and I always liked to go snow-skiing on Spring Break if we were able to!

But, if you'll be at home, Juniors can make excellent use of Spring Break for college research and test prep.

Also, the end of Junior year is usually pretty CRAZY with big tests and projects.

You'll DEFINITELY want to expect at least 50% of your Junior year spring break being devoted to schoolwork and just staying on top of end-of-year projects.

Sophomores and Freshman have a bit less stress during Spring Break, can put the time into free reading and vocabulary!

Spring break is JUST long enough to get your sleep schedule completely screwed-up if you stay up late every night.

One of the biggest RISKS of Spring Break is coming back MORE tired than when you left!

Budget your energy and get good nights of sleep, ESPECIALLY in the few days right before break ends.

Winter Break is actually a much longer holiday than Spring Break...

Although, for some reason I think Spring Break always gets more attention (maybe because it's sunnier or maybe because it's just closer to the end of the school year!)

Juniors MUST make good use of their Winter break to get ahead.

This mainly means SAT and ACT prep as well as a diligent focus on school projects.

It's tempting to relax but honestly, Junior year is SUPPOSED to be super hard since you're showing off your capabilities in preparation for college applications.

If you can push yourself to at least 80% productivity, you won't be TOO stressed over vacation but you will end up with a HUGE amount of important work completed...

Since without school and sports to interfere you should have TONS of time to get ahead if you're a Junior.

Seniors can spend some of Winter break contemplating which college they'll choose if they are accepted to more than one school!

Sophomores and Freshman should do a lot of reading and vocab-building work over Winter break, since it's hard to find so much spare time when school is in session.

Make sure to have plenty of fun and downtime with friends and family and enjoying the excitement of giving and receiving for the Winter holidays!

Finally, please make sure not to get completely loopy with your sleep schedule over Winter Break, which is VERY easy with short days and long nights, plus all the new toys, electronics, or video games you may have after the holidays.

Now, compared to Winter holidays, Thanksgiving Break doesn't offer a whole lot of time to work with.

It's one of those shorter holidays that's mostly just for fun and family.

Use Thanksgiving Break to catch up on small assignments and confirm your winter break plans - there's not enough time to do much else.

Have fun hanging out with family and eating tons of food!

And dont forget one of the best parts of high school - LONG WEEKENDS.

The random long weekends here and there during the school year are a multipurpose mini-vacation that can be used for whatever you need.

It's tempting to use long weekends for purely social things like hanging out with friends, but they are also extremely useful for college visits while school is still in session.

Seniors in particular should be using every long weekend for something productive until their college applications are all sent in.

Juniors - the busiest kids in high school - can, and MUST also use long weekends for extra SAT or ACT prep time.

You don't have to give up the whole weekend in service to test prep, but you have to admit, a 3-day weekend is one of the best possible times to take a practice test and go over your mistakes.

If you haven't already, now's also a great time to put the book down for just a moment and check out our website www.LovetheSAT.com for other online books I've made on test prep and other related topics for high schoolers.

These can give you some great ideas for how to study over a long weekend!

As always, pre-planning and using calendars and journals will enhance your productivity during vacations.

Writing down a daily to-do list and doing end-of-day productivity journaling are probably the bare-minimum effort I would recommend.

But ALSO, holidays deserve some special pre-planning because of how important they are.

What I love to do is use each holiday to plan 1 or 2 holidays ahead, and use SUMMER to plan as much as possible for the entire coming year.

So, for example, you use a little time at the end of your Winter Break to plan and outline your SPRING break.

You use a little time from your SPRING break to plan your SUMMER break.

You use your SUMMER break to GENERALLY outline the next 9 months of your vacation and holiday plans, et cetera.

Make sure to document your intended plans on calendars, computers, or journals - or like me, you can use all three!

Then, put this written-down info somewhere that you will see it often, to remind you of the overall scope of your year.

Planning your high school vacations can take some effort, but here's the good news.

When you're working during the holidays, you get bonus points for productivity.

Just like the weekends, not many people can stick to chasing their dreams when everyone ELSE is being lazy and sleeping in.

So, once you've accomplished a few goals for the day, celebrate!

Don't spend ALL your free time on holiday being productive (unless that's what you truly want to do by choice!)

Actually, I'm not going to lie - sometimes I'm REALLY focused on my business, work, music, or planning and I actually WANT to use my whole holiday to work - but maybe that's just me.

Or maybe, that's the power of FOCUS and discovering your PASSIONS...

In any event, make sure to spend time with family and friends - that's what the holidays are for and we never have enough time for it.

Since the "BIG HOLIDAYS" are one of the only times when EVERYONE has free time, you really want to use at least SOME of that time with the people you care about - even if you are a total workaholic like I am.

So in conclusion, high school vacations and holidays are about balancing the need to recharge, with the urge to get something productive done and not to fall behind the curve.

Sometimes, it's just about enjoying the atmosphere, treats, gifts, and travel that we associate with the holidays.

Other times, it's about motivating yourself to keep moving towards your life goals, instead of just drifting lazily like a spineless jellyfish all summer long.

Many people feel too lazy during the holidays because they SUDDENLY stop doing ANYTHING and then they end up regretting it when the holiday is over - that's NOT actually all that fun!

Instead, find ways to get a jump on your work AND hang out with your family and friends over the holidays.

If you get a jump on the big stuff, you'll have more control over your big-picture YEARLY calendar and this will snowball into lower stress overall in your life.

Last but not least, make sure you take some time to reward yourself for your efforts and enjoy the vacation for what it is - a great chance to get away from high school for a while!

Now I have a fun set of questions for you to answer on Facebook:
(www.Facebook.com/LovetheSAT)**:**

- What's the MOST FUN vacation you've EVER been on?
- Where did you go? WHO did you go with? WHAT did you do?
- Do you have a FAVORITE memory or moment from the trip?

There's nothing that makes me happier than remembering my best trips ever with friends and family.

Take a moment to pause and share your own experience on the Facebook wall **(www.Facebook.com/LovetheSAT)**, and I'll see you in the next lesson!

27. HOW PARENTS CAN HELP

In this chapter, I'd like to touch on a few points that are particularly relevant to parents but also apply to kids as well.

The difficulty of managing schoolwork, test prep, athletics, and college and scholarship applications often leads to tension between parents and kids over time management and scheduling.

Parents are ALREADY busy and shouldn't take on the role of BECOMING a high schooler again.

And meanwhile, students are ultimately responsible for deciding their own destinies.

Although parents can offer a lot of guidance throughout the process, it's ultimately on each kid to take up the role of adulthood and there's no way to FORCE it, only to encourage it.

So parents, please follow the advice of this book - know your OWN "primary purpose" in life, in order to give clarity on how to use YOUR time to help your kid use THEIR time effectively.

YOUR primary purpose as a parent is NOT to live your child's life, but rather to ENABLE it, so consider everything in the light of being an ENABLER not a DOER.

Remember it's about THEM!

As teachers, parents and mentors we can never allow our own fully-developed adult personalities and desires to overshadow the still-growing wants and needs of our students.

Here are a few of my favorite tips for how parents can help ENABLE their kids when it comes to time management:

First of all, help PROTECT your kids' schedules.

High schoolers are simply barraged with opportunities and demands for their time - from book fairs to clubs, climbing trips to cheer teams - the list goes on and on.

Try to clear time for kids to CHOOSE what they WANT to do because they will DEFINITELY have plenty of stuff that they HAVE to do.

I have simply NEVER met a non-busy high schooler, so your first goal should be SUBTRACTION from the schedule, and protecting it from new obligations.

As gatekeepers to the family calendar, this is something parents should always be aware of.

Next, there's a LOT that parents can do to help with "common sense" things that might not be "common sense" to teens yet.

Like leaving on time for commutes and traffic, helping give driving directions, or tips on organization and cleanliness...

Kids often need repeated, kind-hearted reminders on everything from doing their dishes to leaving on time for piano lessons.

DON'T take it personally if you have to repeat yourself with them every week - they are still learning how to manage all the demands on their psyche made by high school and modern life.

It's nearly overwhelming even for battle-hardened ADULTS...

And after all these years of tutoring I actually really deeply RESPECT even the "average" high school student, because every student I've ever met just seems so busy with the rigorous demands on their time and attention.

As a tutor, I also often hear from parents that their teenagers simply won't "hear" advice given by their parents - no matter good the advice is.

Sometimes smart parents come to our tutoring team simply because teenagers usually listen more to OUTSIDE perspectives from NEW sources and teachers they respect.

It's nothing personal - just something about the dynamic of teenagers and parents that seems to be universal and timeless.

So, if you need a little outside help, remember that I love making online books on a wide variety topics that help my students and teenagers, as WELL as their parents.

Please check out the other books and books I've created because I'm sure there will be something there that can help you.

AND, if you have a book idea you WANT me to write, go ahead and let me know via email (Help@LovetheSAT.com)!

I'd be happy to consider your idea for my next book or online course!

Moving on to my next recommendation for parents, I want you to help kids with their SLEEP.

It might sound a little silly to be setting bedtimes at this age, but you have to make sure your teens are going to bed at a reasonable hour.

Make sure they aren't secretly staying up late on computers, video games, TV or social media like my little brother always did!

If there is a computer, laptop or TV in our bedroom it's VERY easy to remain connected and plugged-in 24 / 7, making it much harder to relax and drift to sleep.

The light emitted by screens is also PROVEN to interfere with your brain's sleep chemicals and sleep schedule, but teens may not be fully aware of the implications.

Also understand that occasionally (or perhaps frequently) you will need to serve as the backup alarm clock for your teenager, and this is NORMAL in many families because:

A) High schoolers are overworked,
B) Teenagers' bodies demand a lot of sleep for growth,
C) Teenagers sometimes stay up WAY too late, and
D) Most teenagers aren't great at waking up and getting out of bed... they just aren't.

Homework is a frequent sleep-stealer; so are social media, video games, and surfing the web.

Keep an eye on this stuff and try to balance the need to set limits with the need for kids to make their own decisions and have some fun free time.

On a similar note, help kids with *balance*. Keep them from getting overloaded in any one direction.

Sports, academics, hobbies, health - all have their place.

Try to prevent any unhealthy obsessions from taking root, and help kids see their weak AND strong points with clarity and empathy.

Talk to your kids. Find out what is on their mind, if you can, without PRYING or making them feel self-conscious.

It's not easy, but no one ever said being a parent was!

I just want to say, if you're a parent of a high school student, you REALLY impress me and I'm here to help any way I can.

Try to help with PEER PRESSURE but ALSO - recognize the INSANE amount of importance that social life has to high schoolers because you have to respect it for what it is.

For many kids in high school, the opinion of their peers is LIFE OR DEATH - it means the world to them.

Understand that this may be the source of some pushback you receive when it comes to scheduling and time management.

As an adult, it can be tough to empathize but try to see matters from your own eyes when you were 15, 16 or 17.

BE there for your kids - let them know you are - and always remind them; but don't be too pushy.

Try to let them CHOOSE when they come to you for help - this shows how much you respect them and it will help them build their confidence.

As a parent, try to BE the BACKUP PLAN for your teenagers, but don't TELL them you're the backup plan.

On important matters related to time management or scheduling, don't let them KNOW that you have a "Plan B" ready, and MINIMIZE INTERFERENCE.

But, if your kid stumbles or makes a mistake, you can be ready to step in and lend a hand to prevent disaster - WITHOUT taking over their life.

High schoolers are often VERY smart, but weak with the long-term perspective in life.

Don't blame them! They are still developing and it's impossible for them to have a complete perspective of life at the age of 16 or 17.

Help them figure out what their time is best used for, without FORCING your personality on them.

For most of us, COLLEGE is usually the "obvious" big goal, BUT - PERSONAL FULFILLMENT is the true long-term goal.

And surprisingly, that's often lost and forgotten in the scheme of things as everyone jockeys for position to get into college.

With that in mind, remember that your kid's definition of ultimate success is very probably different than yours - sometimes a *little* different and sometimes a *lot* different -

And quite possibly your kid DOESN"T EVEN KNOW YET what their definition of success is.

Again don't blame them, they are only 16 or 17 and simply haven't had the chance to get the breadth of experiences that an adult has.

Therefore, the MOST important "true goal" parents can focus on to help is ENABLE their kids to DISCOVER their true selves and the passions that will drive them through college, career and adult life.

It's easy to run around like mad following "prescribed" important tasks, resume, agenda that we're "supposed" to be doing according to society.

But the impossible task of trying to make society pleased with us can OFTEN lead to unhappiness in both the short term and the long run.

ALWAYS feel free to "rewrite the social rules" for your kid - when it comes to the long game of life, happiness and fulfillment matter *so, so* much more than any external definition of sucesss.

So - listen to what your kids are SAYING about their schedules, and their time and energy - not what you THINK they should be saying!

Deep down, we all know this already, because we love the kids and students we're here to help and guide...

But it's easy to forget in the midst of our competitive culture that forces us to feel like we're keeping up with the Joneses - a culture that turns our KIDS into COMMODITIES.

Never let the rat race get the best of you or most ESPECIALLY your kids and their dreams.

ALWAYS keep passion, fun, fulfillment, and happiness as your central goals - NOT money or prestige or fame in the eyes of others.

This goes double when it comes to our students and teens who often need more time to figure out who they are.

Let's help protect their schedules and enable them to try, succeed, and fail on their own merits...

So that over time they grow into young adults who WANT to manage, and CHOOSE to manage their time efficiently without the need for our oversight -

Because they have big goals and big dreams that they want to accomplish on their OWN and they don't NEED us to get them done!

Thats what I think. But, I've never actually BEEN a parent, just a teacher. So, what do YOU think the role of a parent should be?

How much should they be involved in their teenager's high school schedule and time management?

Is high school a time for parents to control and lead the schedule, using the benefit of their more mature perspective to make wise choices?

OR, is high school intended as a time for students to make their OWN mistakes and learn to live independently?

I can see it going either way, so I want to know what the students and parents reading this book think.

So please take a moment to head to the Facebook page (www.Facebook.com/LovetheSAT) to describe the IDEAL role of a parent or guardian and how involved they should be in their teenager's schedule and schoolwork.

There's no wrong answer, I just want your feedback on Facebook, and afterwards I'll see you in the next lesson!

28. THE BEST BOOKS ON HIGH SCHOOL TIME MANAGEMENT

Remember in the previous section, we covered some of the best-ever CLASSIC time management books that are full of relevant tips no matter WHO you are or what age you are.

In this chapter we're going to do the same thing, but with 3 books oriented around HIGH SCHOOL time management because you know that's what we're completely focused on right now!

These books are all available on Amazon.com and can be read by students or parents (or better yet, both!) and discussed as a family.

OF COURSE, please remember to take NOTES on them as you read in order to increase your memory and ultimately save tons of time in life!

We're going to hit the best three books this time - and in no particular order, here's the quick list:

- The Organized Student by Donna Goldberg
- Smart but Scattered Teens by Richard Guare
- 50 Tips to Help Your Student Succeed by Marydee Sklar

First up we have The Organized Student: Teaching Children the Skills for Success in School and Beyond by Donna Goldberg.

This book has a wide variety of applications - it's written towards parents of middle school and high school kids but can easily be read and used by students on their own.

Particularly good for kids who are really disorganized, inconsistent with completing and turning assignments, or who might be considered to have ADD or ADHD -

And, for what it's worth, this pretty much describes *exactly* the kid I was in high school!

With an average 4.5 star review on Amazon and 79 customer reviews it's one of the most popular books on the subject for teens.

Up next we've got Smart but Scattered Teens: The "Executive Skills" Program for Helping Teens Reach Their Potential, by Richard Guare and Peg Dawson.

This is actually the #1-selling book on Amazon in TWO categories of Adolescent Psychology, which basically means it's VERY popular for helping teens with some common struggles.

As the book title says it's all about helping disorganized teens reach their potential.

It's a excellent read for students AND parents and was written with the really COMPASSIONATE and COOL aim of improving the lives of kids, parents and families and bringing them closer together – and deep down that is something I know that we all want.

You can also download free additional forms and worksheets with this book to make the experience even more effective.

Last but not least, check out 50 Tips to Help Students Succeed: Develop Your Time-Management and Executive Skills for Life, by Marydee Sklar.

This one is MAINLY focused towards parents -

However it's got a lot of popularity within its niche, and I wanted to include it for particularly-mature high schoolers who recognize that they could benefit from some additional outside counseling on time management.

Those who read this book will come away with tips to overcome resistance over the assignments and chores that MUST be done anyway -

Which is excellent preparation for life, the working world, and in my own experience, entrepreneurship or starting up ANY independent project or team...

Because when you get out on your own after college, all your success depends on your ability to set your own goals and decide ON YOUR OWN how you will reach them and then to GO AFTER them.

I don't mean to make it sound over-dramatic, but this is one of those books that talks seriously about how teens can get over our urges to procrastinate and resist doing work that obviously must be done, even we aren't exactly looking forward to that work.

That's my short list of three top high-school time management books, but if I can just state the obvious, reading another book isn't going to solve your time crunch or motivation problems.

What you need most is to follow the three primary rules of time management so that you're consistently working towards a set of life goals that matter to you.

However, the more you LEARN, the more you absorb from the experts, and other people who have been down this road, the better prepared you become -

And getting new author's perspectives and insights is ALWAYS a good thing to help you develop.

Remember, all of these books are easily available on Amazon.com.

I wouldn't consider them "essential" to being a great high school student, but they are excellent supplements to your work so far and are also preparation for college.

Take a look and see which titles you like - you can order one or two at same time as your order some of the other "classic" time management books from our previous reading list chapter.

This is also a great time to throw in some physical planners and wall calendars to the shopping cart, so take a moment to pause the chapter and order your supplemental materials, journals, and books if you haven't done so already.

OH! By the way, if you like my teaching style, you can also find more of my OWN books for high schoolers on Amazon.com if you search for me as "Christian Heath" or "Love the SAT."

And, plenty of other new books coming as well since I'm always writing more.

SO readers, do YOU have any other book recommendations?

I'd love to know them - please take a second to share them on the Facebook wall! (www.Facebook.com/LovetheSAT)

Honestly, I'm down for ANY book recommendations - even if it's NOT about time management and it's just a great book for high schoolers.

Leave the book title and author name for me on the Facebook page and I'll see you in the next chapter!

29. A PREVIEW OF COLLEGE-LEVEL TIME MANAGEMENT

THIS chapter previewing college-level time management and lifestyle is one I really enjoyed writing, because for me, college was a difficult but a VERY rewarding time.

It's where I discovered new limits for myself and made huge steps towards discovering what I truly love about being alive.

We're going to cover a LOT of ground in this chapter, but my main goal is for you, as a high schooler, to know more about what the POINT of college really is...

And to get an overview of how college is actually a lot like high school but at the same time, totally.. totally.. different.

And much better. In my opinion college is MUCH better than high school, so I hope that's something for you to look forward to.

This all is CENTRAL to time management because as you will learn throughout this chapter, college is a period where you must NATURALLY become better at organizing yourself.

But interestingly, it's actually much EASIER to manage your time in college, IF you follow my advice of FIRST uncovering some of what you LOVE and what you want to DO with your life.

We're going to talk about all this and more in the coming pages, so get your pen and paper ready!

I thought we could start off with a quick discussion of some of the main SIMILARITIES between college and high school as you know it.

So what's the SAME from high school to college?

Well, there's still the same "juggling" feeling as many other activities and many other distractions compete for your time and attention - except in college it's even more intense.

Because of all the possible uses of your time, motivating yourself to study still takes just as much effort as it does in high school.

You'll probably still want a social life which means you still need to find your clique and who you sit with at lunch, so to speak, all over again - which takes time.

You still need to maintain yourself and your life, which means feeding yourself, bathing yourself, sleeping, and stuff like that, except NOW you'll be responsible for doing it all on your own, including the much-dreaded laundry!!

Homework is still probably one of your biggest hassles in college and yes, there is tons of homework.

Of book, just like in high school, you'll find that some college classes are more like blow-offs, while some other classes will be NOTORIOUSLY difficult or have a super-strict professor.

There's also a wide range of students in every college: from hardworking to lazy, from friendly to jerks - just the same as in high school.

Last but not least, final exams and final projects are still a "thing" only now they hit even harder than before - often counting for a huge percent of your final grade.

So as you can imagine, many elements of college can be surprisingly SIMILAR to high school - although usually a lot more INTENSE.

Now, there are equally as many DIFFERENCES between college and high school.

One of the BIGGEST and MOST important things to realize is that college has fewer "GUARDRAILS" than high school does.

Your PARENTS aren't there, and even if they seem like they're always ordering around all through high school, the HONEST TRUTH is that they're just trying to help you make smart decisions.

You set up your own study schedule in college without oversight and there's very little guidance unless you go seeking it on your own.

There is MUCH more distraction in college - probably one hundred more times as many ways to procrastinate.

The thing is, without parental supervision, no one will STOP you from wasting an entire semester and then FLUNKING OUT of three classes and losing your scholarship.

That's what's a little scary - you might not have a whole lot of "warning signs" along the way, and big problems can come up if you're not ready for a major college-level test because the book will just keep rolling along without you.

Even the "easy" college classes are a lot of WORK - basically every book has tons of stuff to DO, so whether the assignments are EASY or HARD - they will still be TIME CONSUMING.

At the same time, you are given less GUIDANCE on how to ACCOMPLISH your assignments.

Basically you're thrown into the deep end, and it's YOUR responsibility to figure out how to use the library outside of class, for example=.

It's not just your classes and homework, though - your college lifestyle requires more independence in EVERY aspect of life, from attending classes to feeding yourself.

You'll have to find time to eat, and hopefully eat HEALTHY - easier said than done!

It's also highly likely that you're in a new city or even a new state so seemingly simple chores and errands can take more of your time.

You might even have to deal with SNOW for the first time, if you're from the south and went to a school up north!

Imagine how that could slow you down as you're going about your day, trying to figure everything out and get your assignments done while still managing your personal and social life - and there's two feet of SNOW everywhere!

College can definitely put you in some pretty weird and new situations - but then again, that's part of the fun.

On the slightly less-fun side, you might feel more isolated since there's less organization forcing people to interact and team up the way you do now in high school.

In other words, college requires you to make a SERIOUS social effort if you want to be noticed, find your ideal friend group and stand out among them -

Because EVERYONE in college is so distracted with their own stuff, you really have to put effort into social time as well...

Unlike high school where everyone ends up hanging out on campus together during study halls because there's literally nothing else to do and you're not allowed to leave school.

Both the THRILL and the RISK of college come from the fast that there is a very

REAL risk of failure and you absolutely CAN flunk out of college if you don't put in the effort.

At university YOU are expected to either:

A) Solve your own problems, or
B) HAVE THE COMMON SENSE to seek out and locate help.

In high school, you're monitored enough that an adult would usually notice you were struggling and try to help somehow -

But in college, most likely no one will be watching out for you so closely unless you TELL them you need help.

Of book we could keep going and find MILLIONS of tiny little differences and similarities between time management in high school and college...

But I think this suffices to show the GENERAL outline of how high school and college are different.

So, I wanted to leave abstract lists and comparisons behind, and share a bit from my OWN life on MY four years in college and the transformation I went through as I responded to the new pressures and challenges of college.

For me, Freshman year was filled with time-wasting parties, getting to know my fellow students -

I was taking required classes, discovering what I liked to study, adjusting to new levels of homework, projects, science labs, and tests, and learning to manage my time and my newfound freedom.

I kept trying things that interested me, and by the end of the year, I had discovered a real PASSION when I came back to piano and classical music which I hadn't really studied for a few years.

Over the summer after freshman year, I continued to spend more and more of my free time on music and practice - realizing more and more that I REALLY wanted to go further in it.

That marked a transition point for me, because by the time I came back to college as a sophomore I was much more serious about studying music.

I started buckling down - cutting the fat, skipping parties I didn't really care about.

Instead I was preparing for high-level piano performances, taking specialized classes in music history and composition, deciding who I WANTED to be and as a result, natural leadership positions and momentum started building for me.

By the time I was a Junior in college, I was in full-on commitment mode;

I was partying rarely, if at all; I needed to focus my health and even my DIET towards supporting my passion and schedule for music.

I get a paying job as a music librarian, allowing me to continue to study and learn even while I was at work - that's just one easy example of how everything can continue to focus around your central passion, *once you know what it IS*.

Often working the equivalent of 80-hour and even 120-hour work-weeks in the practice rooms and in my studies, I also experienced massive failure on multiple levels as I attempted push myself beyond my limits.

For example, because I'd taken on too many competing demands, I ended up forgetting the music in the middle of a solo performance in front of the entire music department, which was really embarrassing at the time.

Despite a few major failures, there were FAR more successes and a general feeling of progress towards something I cared about, and the people around me seemed positively influenced by my focus as well.

Everything culminated in senior year with a sense of calm and purpose.

Even though I was working even HARDER than I had junior year, somehow I feel more peaceful throughout senior year.

I continued to cut out bad habits that slowed me down because I was so focused on my goal of my senior recital, the final performance.

It wasn't hard at this point to prioritize my choices and decisions because my path is incredibly clear to me.

I was also engaged in multiple leadership roles and music groups, and my help is sought by both other students and faculty on campus who want to do music-related stuff for their OWN goals or projects..

I got the chance to play in front of the biggest crowds of my life, and the year brought a mix of success and failure again since I was attempting to push myself beyond my limits,

But this time I had a better estimation of my limits than last year.

Each time you go beyond your current limits, you learn so much more about your true strength level - even if you fail!

And college is the perfect place for low-risk failure and learning experiences.

At the very end of senior year, I won the most prestigious solo competition on campus, and gave multiple performances that I'm still proud of.

So because of my single-minded focus I was able to wisely prioritize my time because I really CARED about what I was working on and working towards.

Fast forward about five years, and although it's been several years since I've worked on music as much as I did in college, the work ethic has remained.

My passion for music and art has ALSO retained an INCREDIBLE power to motivate me and one of my major life goals is still to produce music in multiple forms that I can share with other people.

In many ways, learning to control my schedule and lead a team of fellow musicians was the PERFECT training for starting a small tutoring business.

To this day, I'm thankful for the effort I put in and the chances I took in college - if anything, I would only do *more* of that if I could go back and do it all over.

I'd put in MORE effort. MORE risk-taking. MORE discovering my limits through failure, and MORE pushing on to find what I truly love about being alive.

But overall, I'd say I feel very proud of my results and education throughout my four years in college.

So again, it's just one of those things where I'm hoping to pass it on or pay it forward or whatever you want to call it and just SHARE this important information that I feel like I'm lucky to know about.

So, what's the recipe to make it work for you throughout college?

Here are my 3 tips that I'd give to *myself* if I could go back in time, and instead I'll pass on to you!

First, START TRYING IN HIGH SCHOOL to discover your true passions, instead of waiting till college to start -

There's no perfect way to do this, but if you DON'T even try it's just so JARRING when you get to college because it's TOUGH and BUSY and INDEPENDENT...

And if you don't really CARE about what you're supposed to be doing, you may FAIL and you will CERTAINLY underperform because you won't really care about your studies.

And that's exactly how and why you hear about people flunking out of college even when they seemed so promising.

Most of the time, they just didn't really know why they were THERE.

Second, as much as possible, identify and stay focused around what matters to YOU -

It was MUCH easier to handle the stress and find the energy and time in college for MUSIC because I LOVED it;

And I LOVED playing the piano, and getting better at it (whether or not ANYONE even heard me) and highly valued the whole process...

So my efforts aligned with my values, and that's EXACTLY why I could work massive 12 to 14 hour days for my studies when I needed to.

When you hear about people who work insanely hard, and it seems superhuman, it's ONLY because they care SO MUCH about what they're doing that they don't even THINK about it -

They just HAVE to keep doing it and then it doesn't even feel like WORK.

Again, this is the SECRET of time management - as long as you're working on things you DON'T care about, you will STRUGGLE to control your time.

So, tip three: dip your toes in a LOT of possible activities in college, as soon as possible.

Try many different clubs, different social groups, and seek out new experiences continually.

Forcing yourself out of your comfort zone will definitely give you new ideas - but amidst all your sampling, only COMMIT to a FEW things!!

Be SELFISH with your COMMITMENTS, but generous with your "first times."

Be the type of person who will try anything at least once and you will have a great time in college.

So, I hope you're really looking FORWARD to this part of your life.

The same lessons of life management continue to apply - discover your passions, and use them to naturally power up your strength and abilities.

It's true that college demands a wiser and more diligent approach if you want to rise to the top...

But the REAL secret, as always, is to discover what makes you WANT to sit down and study - to focus - or practice - and to IMPROVE in some way towards your favorite personal goals.

When you get to college as a freshman, you might learn similar lessons to the ones that I learned.

For example, partying might seem fun in the moment, but I think it takes you away from what you TRULY care about...

... Your most important life's work, the things that will bring you peace and fulfillment and a sense of meaning.

Don't let partying distract you for too long. Allow college to transform you and help you get closer to your dreams!

So, what do YOU hope to study in college? What's the topic that's going to deserve YOUR focus and study?

Is there some major, college book, or study program that you get REALLY excited for? Let me know on the Facebook page! (www.Facebook.com/LovetheSAT)

Or, do you feel like you have NO idea what you're truly passionate about?

Either way, pause for a moment to drop me a line on Facebook and I'll see you in the next chapter!

Additional Reading:
www.LovetheSAT.com/top-tips-to-get-good-grades-in-college

QUIZ #4: REVIEW OF TIME MANAGEMENT FOR HIGH SCHOOLERS

Welcome to the fourth quiz of Ultimate Time Management for Teens and Students!

Remember, it's all about memory and recall.

There's no time limit. Go slowly and try to get them all correct.

Answers are on p.190.

QUESTION #1: When is "too early" for a high schooler to begin test prep for the SAT and ACT tests?

A) 9th grade is too early.
B) 10th grade is too early.
C) 11th grade is too early.
D) There's no such thing as "too early" when it comes to SAT / ACT prep.

QUESTION #2: Spending 12 to 18 months or MORE on your COLLEGE and SCHOLARSHIPS search is...

A) Totally crazy.
B) Kinda crazy.
C) Not crazy at all.

QUESTION #3: If you're doing an activity that you DO NOT enjoy and that does NOT teach you anything, you should:

A) Stick it out - there may be a lesson in the end.
B) Cut it out of your schedule the moment you get bored - everything you spend time on should always be interesting to you.
C) Ask yourself if there's a hidden payoff that makes this activity worth the effort; if not, strongly consider quitting in the near future and replacing it with a new activity that you like better.

QUESTION #4: When it comes to time management and personal fulfillment, PEER PRESSURE in high school can lead to...

A) The occasional fun time and crazy memory with your friends (as long as you don't get caught).
B) REALLY STUPID personal decisions that harm us later in life when we don't live up to our potential.
C) Wasting time instead of completing important assignments and studying.
D) Doing things that don't really interest you or make you feel fulfilled, just to fit in.
E) All of the above.

QUESTION #5: The most common risk of study groups in high school is:

A) Not being able to find a good PLACE to study.
B) Not being able to find a good TIME for everyone to meet.
C) Having a social hour but calling it a "Study Group."
D) There's no risk - study groups are ALWAYS a good thing in high school.

QUESTION #6: Weekends in high school are an ideal time to:

A) Finally do NOTHING after all your rushing around during the week - just kick back and relax Friday to Monday morning.
B) A 50/50 blend of relaxing and working - particularly on the biggest yearly goals like test prep, college apps, major tests and projects.
C) Keep trying to work full-tilt, 100% steam ahead! This is how you get ahead of the competition.
D) Forget completely about school and college - take some time to focus on YOURSELF and your favorite activities and shut out the rest of the world.

QUESTION #7: According to my theory, why do so many people (students AND adults) feel bad during, and after, the holidays when it comes to time management?

A) They eat too much, and generally overindulge, leading to stomach aches during the holidays that distract them from working.
B) After being hardworking in school or work, many people get really lazy over the holidays and then are mad at themselves for not using the free time to get any closer to their true personal dreams.
C) They feel guilty for not picking the best gifts for everyone.
D) The holidays are a time when more people commonly get sick - illnesses like the flu or mono are often going around during these times of year and you have to plan ahead for it.

QUESTION #8: The MOST important ways parents can help their teens with scheduling, productivity, and time management is:

A) Protect and enable kids to DISCOVER their true passions that will drive them through college, career and adult life.
B) Take control of the family schedule at the start of each school year, preventing obvious mistakes that teenagers often make due to inexperience.
C) Take a hands-off approach and allow students to learn entirely on the basis of their own successes and failures. Experience is the best teacher.
D) Always tell your kids you have a plan B ready for them when they fail, so that they won't feel as pressured to get things right the first time.

QUESTION #9: Which of these short stories approximately describes MY college experience?

A) Freshman year very lonely; Sophomore year I found my friend group and had a great time; Junior year I started questioning my passions; Senior year I studied business and started my first company.
B) Freshman year I studied music; Sophomore year I switched to medicine; Junior and Senior year I pushed myself to the limit with an internship and a double degree in science and health.
C) Freshman year parties; Sophomore year more serious; Junior year very hard-working and was taking on leadership in my department; Senior year extremely focused and took multiple leadership positions and awards.

ANSWERS ON p.190.

30. REVIEW OF MAIN THEMES FOR HIGH SCHOOLERS

WOW, welcome to the final review section of this book on time management for teenagers and THANK YOU from the bottom of my heart for joining me to read it - I really don't feel like I can say "THANK YOU" enough!

I feel SO lucky to have students like you taking my online video courses, reading our books and blog posts, and studying with us at Love the SAT.

Every good book should contain a review section, so that's what this chapter is all about.

I hope you've been taking great notes along the way, but here are some of the highlights of what we covered!

First you got to know me and my own desperate personal need to balance time between multiple commitments like teaching, business management, motorcycling, music, family, friends, continual learning, and coming up with new ideas and projects as well as keeping myself healthy and happy.

Then we dove into a section on TIMELESS, eternal principles of good time management.

For example, in a very early chapter, we covered 3 timeless rules of time management - do you remember what they are?

We devoted a lot of time to identifying our top priorities or at least working TOWARDS knowing our top priorities.

I've heavily recommended the use of JOURNALS, daily planners, and physical calendars to gain insight and control over your schedule and daily energy because nothing beats the insights of a handwritten, visual representation of your schedule that YOU have made yourself.

I also went into some of my theories and personal themes about the rhythms of life and how to organize the cycles of your life to provide momentum and rhythm on every dimension from the hourly to the yearly levle.

I recommended that you monitor and manage your health, exercise, and sleep - because NOTHING wastes more time than being sick in bed.

To help keep you motivated during all this hard work, I included some great quotes and books on the subject since this is something EVERYONE, literally EVERY human being, has to think about so it's interesting and useful to see how OTHER experts have handled the topic of time management.

After hitting the timeless principles, then we focused in on high school itself.

With an eye towards your high school classes, we covered how to take notes, make and use flashcards, get to know your teachers personally, and an assortment of other specific tricks to save time on your assignments.

You now know that you want to first plan each semester around predictable, important events: finals, SAT/ACT testing, college apps and essays, family vacations, college tours, sports, extracurriculars and other major events.

Then fill in the days and weeks with fun and resume-boosting activities that fit you - using high school and college as the perfect times to seek out the top ONE to FIVE goals that will DEFINE you in life.

That may be a big goal, but on the way there, even the little things matter - like creating a cozy, clean and organized quiet study space - especially because technology fights for your attention and time, now more than ever.

Speaking of that, control over distracting technology (AND useful technology) is going to rapidly separate strong and weak students in the future...

Because some students will MULTIPLY their time and effectiveness with technology and computers; while other students will WASTE massive amounts of their own time on technology and computers.

We also covered social aspects of time management, like finding time for your friends amidst all the pre-college pressures - as well as harmful aspects of peer pressure that can waste your time and cost you big down the road.

Rounding things out was a preview of college-level time management and some of the challenges that you will face at that point, as well as some advantages to preparing for your busy college rhythms in advance.

Now, when it comes to the SPECIFICS, you can use my models and follow my advice, or you can carve your own path -

But what matters most to me the MOST is that you understand the need to be USING your time here on earth to do what MATTERS to you, or at the very least to work TOWARDS what matters to you and get closer day by day.

THAT'S the true motivation behind why I spent the MONTHS it took me to create this book -

Because I think it would make the world a better place if we all were a little more productive on the things that we really cared about.

All in all, here's the short version of ALL the themes of the book:

A well-ordered, productive, successful, and fun life doesn't just happen by accident.

Starting in high school, you need to sit down and deliberately prepare a personal approach to handle all the different demands on your time, without going crazy.

Our ability to manage our time and organize ALL our efforts in life around a few central goals that matter most to us is often what makes the difference between what we call success and what we call failure.

And, I KNOW that as soon you identify your central goals and work towards them with all your strength and speed...

At that moment, you will not only know the TRUE meaning of "feeling fulfilled," you will also find the majority of your time management problems and anxieties DISAPPEARING -

Because the strength of your personal convictions will BURN them away as you walk your true path in life.

Now that we're almost at the end of the book, I wanted to ask you this INCREDIBLY important question -

What's the NUMBER ONE biggest thing you've learned from reading this book?

Please share it on the Facebook wall (www.Facebook.com/LovetheSAT) because I am DYING to know what you will take away from our time together.

Or, if there's something you WANTED to learn about, but didn't, please share THAT too on the Facebook page and maybe I can add a bonus chapter or blog article about the topic!

Leave a quick note about your BIGGEST lesson or question, and I'll see you in our last few chapters to wrap things up.

31. WHAT TO DO NEXT

All throughout the book I've been giving you tons of stuff to DO and THINK ABOUT so in a way it seems kind of unnecessary to make a specific "Action Steps" chapter at the end, which is the way I USUALLY end my books and online courses.

But, I still thought I'd boil things down and give you a few ideas of what to do RIGHT NOW if you don't think you're ready to go it alone.

First of all, go back and review the written notes you've taken on this book.

Hopefully you've taken some good notes, and if not I want you to try again in the near future, because you'll get so much more out of the whole learning experience if you do.

Also, make sure you've taken all the QUIZZES in the book and read the supplementary BLOG ARTICLES at www.LovetheSAT.com/blog and elsewhere throughout the internet.

And, get onto Amazon.com and order any book recommendations you liked throughout the book (AND any of MY other books that you want to read next).

Read your new books and take notes on them just like you hopefully did with THESE lessons.

At the same time you can also order your calendars and planners and start using them as soon as they arrive.

Mark down the most important dates of the next 6 to 24 months. Start with the obvious major events like finals, SAT/ACT tests, college apps, sports, and family vacations.

Get in the habit of creating a to-do list each morning, or the night before, if you haven't already.

DEFINITELY make sure you're keeping an end-of-the-day journal, no matter HOW simple or short your entries are each day.

Keep a careful eye on your use of technology.

Figure out how to use technology to your advantage and prevent it from harming you through its power to distract and waste your time.

And, share and discuss the lessons you've learned here.

Whether you're a student or a parent, TALK to your family and friends about the lessons of this book and figure out how you can HELP each other based on your personal strong and weak points.

Last but not least, set a time on your yearly calendar, six to twelve months from now, to read the book AGAIN from a new and more mature perspective, because you will definitely notice NEW things to work on each time you re-watch the book.

You should keep the book for life, and I want you to take advantage of that access to review the book from time to time as you grow up.

To put the finishing touches on our time together, here are a few final steps:

One, it REALLY helps me to get honest reviews and feedback. They help my business grow and they help ME grow as an author and instructor.

I'm ALWAYS deeply grateful for your ratings and feedback. So PLEASE, make sure you've left a review and some honest personal feedback for me on this book!

The #1 best place to leave a review is on the book page at Amazon.com – just search up Ultimate Time Management for Teens and give it your seal of approval! (or tell me what to improve, or both!)

The #2 best place to tell me what you think is the Facebook page!

Two, use the Facebook page (www.Facebook.com/LovetheSAT) for ANY questions you have about ANYTHING we covered in the book and I will answer.

Three, reread this book, in whole or in part, any time you want – I want you to keep it for LIFE because I want you to return and reflect on these lessons as you grow.

If you had a good time and learned a lot in the book, please keep studying with me!

This DEFINITELY shouldn't be the last time we study together.

I, and the team of tutors at Love the SAT Test Prep, have written hundreds of articles, made dozens of videos, and taught hundreds and hundreds of high school students in person -

We're creating an AWESOME collection of online courses, books and ebooks, and video content, and we are constantly adding new stuff every month!

If you've had a good time studying with me, check out my other online courses and books at www.LovetheSAT.com or on Amazon.com, and enroll in any that strike your fancy.

Also visit our main website Love the SAT.com, where you can **join the free mailing list for free bonus reports on SAT / ACT prep, exclusive study tips to help you get into college and much more.**

You can also find and follow us on social media, especially:
- Facebook (www.Facebook.com/LovetheSAT)
- Twitter, (@LovetheSAT) and
- YouTube (Search for "Love the SAT")

We use social media to post a ton more exclusive high school, test prep, and college readiness-related content on a daily basis, just for you.

As always, if you have questions related to this book, please use the Facebook wall to ask me what you're wondering about and I'll personally respond as soon as I can.

Thanks again for studying with me and I hope to hear from you and see you again soon!

32. LEAVE A REVIEW / CONTACT ME!

Well, that's it for this book on high school time management!

Thanks again SO MUCH for studying with me, because I've had a REALLY great time making it the whole way through.

Just by CREATING this book, I feel like I've been showered with new and useful insights about how I can improve my OWN time management, and continue to mature and grow towards my OWN life purpose - the same exact thing I want most for my students.

Now - if you feel like helping ME out a TON, it would be SO awesome if you could give me some feedback by leaving a book review through Amazon.com feedback system.

Not only does honest feedback help me improve this book and others I make in the future - meaning that YOU will have access to better and better books and courses by leaving me honest feedback...

It ALSO helps me get discovered by new students who could benefit from this stuff, and THAT helps me grow my business which is REALLY important to me personally.

So, if you've loved it, hated it - please leave me a review!

The more information the better... If you can just leave a star rating, great!

Or even better, leave some details and thoughts about the book!

Was the book too fast? Too slow? Did it have too many new ideas? Or was there too much repetition?

Did you like my personality and tone as an author? Did it seem like I knew what I was talking about, and that I CARED about you as my student?

What sort of actionable lessons or tricks did you take away? What MINDSET shifts did you experience as you took the book?

Did you find the supplemental blog reading useful? Were the quizzes appropriately challenging and engaging?

These are ALL topics I'd be happy to hear about.

If you struggle for ideas, don't worry, it's easy. Literally ANY feedback or commentary you provide will be useful.

So whatever pops into your head right now is EXACTLY what I want to know in your review.

Any lessons you learned, improvements you can think of...

Or if there's stuff you wanted to know MORE about...

Maybe if you thought my writing style could improve, or the quality of the book printing...

Any of that info would be SUPER-helpful for you to leave in a book review on Amazon.com, because then I can take that advice and improve for next time.

Now, I'm almost completely done but I have another quick announcement to make.

There are a TON of topics that I want to help you out with if you're a teenager or high schooler or the parent or guardian of one!

I have published OTHER online courses, books and ebooks for high schoolers and parents and I'm adding more all the time.

My normal audience is anyone who is what you might call "pre-college-prep" or "ambitious high school student" - as well as the PARENTS of these students.

I ALSO have a soft spot for kids and parents who AREN'T as ambitious but just want to do a little better in school.

So whether your goals for high school and college are AMBITIOUS or more MODEST...

If that's YOU, then I have been thinking NON-STOP about what other topics and useful lessons I can teach you.

Since my company specializes in SAT / ACT prep, college counseling, and academic excellence in high school and college, I can pretty much GUARANTEE that you're going to find more books that are REALLY helpful for you.

From study skills and test prep, to college and scholarship applications, we're constantly expanding the RANGE and the QUALITY of our collection of online courses and textbooks for pre-college high schoolers and parents.

So, if you're interested in checking out the other topics, WHERE can you find these other books classes?

Well, just head over to our book store at www.LovetheSAT.com or search for me on Amazon (remember, my name is Christian Heath) and you'll be able to see all the other books and courses that I've done.

Go look right now and enroll in your next favorite class with me!

One last thing - please get in touch with me if there's anything you need!

You have your choice of how to do it - you can reach out to us on Facebook... (www.Facebook.com/LovetheSAT)

Or, send us an email (Help@LovetheSAT.com).

Or contact us through the Love the SAT website (www.LovetheSAT.com).

And, if you want, you can even study with our team personally! We teach in-person lessons at our headquarters in Austin, Texas...

And we also offer premium, 1-on-1 LIVE online tutoring to students anywhere in the world via high-speed videoconferencing and chat.

We usually set that up via email (again, Help@LovetheSAT.com), so just drop us a line if you're interested in learning more.

As always, if you have any questions related to the subject matter of this book, you can also use the discussion section so that all students and instructors can see it.

So to wrap things up - for REAL:

1. One, leave me a review on the book and what you thought of it.
2. Two, send me a note (in some form) about how you're doing and what you need more help with.
3. Third, find our other online courses and books and enroll in them, and
4. Fourth, get to work on your time management skills!

Most of all, please uncover what makes you HAPPY to do in life and spend as many hours as possible doing it.

Thanks again for joining me and see you in our next book or course together,

**This is Christian from Love the SAT Test Prep,
Signing off for now.**

QUIZ #5: REVIEW OF THE CONCLUSION

Welcome to the fifth and final quiz of Ultimate Time Management for Teens and Students! I hope they've been helpful, and that you've learned more and felt more engaged with the book!

Remember, the quizzes are all about memory and recall.

There's no time limit. Go slowly and try to get them all correct.

Answers are on p.191.

QUESTION #1: What's the number-one thing you learned from this course?

A) I already told you! I already put that on the Facebook wall!
(www.Facebook.com/LovetheSAT)
B) I'm still thinking...

QUESTION #2: What's the first action step to take, immediately after finishing this course?

A) Review your course notes.
B) Order more books and online courses at Love the SAT.com.
C) Get into college.
D) Go watch some T.V. to relax.

QUESTION #3: Have you looked through my other books and video courses for teens, students, high school, college, and parents?

A) No, I haven't looked yet at your other books or video courses yet!
B) I've looked through your books, but not your other courses!
C) I've looked through your other courses, but not the books!
D) Yeah! I've seen your other courses AND your other books!

QUESTION #4: Have you left a Book Review and feedback for <u>Ultimate Time Management for Teens and Students</u> on Amazon.com?

A) Yes, I've left a book review and feedback!
B) Almost...
C) Nope.

QUESTION #5: What's the best way to contact me now that you've finished the book?

A) By leaving an Amazon.com book review.
B) Email (<u>Help@LovetheSAT.com</u>)
C) Web (<u>www.LovetheSAT.com/Contact_Us</u>)
D) Facebook (<u>www.Facebook.com/LovetheSAT</u>)
E) Twitter (@LovetheSAT)
F) All of the above!

ANSWERS ON p.191.

ANSWERS TO QUIZZES

Quiz #1: Review of the Introduction (p. 11)

1. **A -** That's right! My name is Christian :)
2. **C -** Yes! I'm from Love the SAT Test Prep!
3. **C –** You got it! The name of this book is <u>Ultimate Time Management for Teens and Students</u>.
4. **A -** Yup - if you're a busy high school student, then you're in EXACTLY the right place right now!
5. **C –** Exactly! Notes help your memory and recall – saving you time in the long run. Also you need them for college!
6. **D –** All of the above! You can contact us in ANY way that works for you. Email (<u>Help@LovetheSAT.com</u>), <u>website</u>, <u>Facebook</u>, or otherwise.
7. **A -** Excellent! Setting a completion date will help you finish quickly and practice your time-management skills, and *sharing* your deadline on the Facebook wall will give you a social reason to follow up on your promise.

How did you do on Quiz #1? Share your results and questions on the Facebook wall (<u>www.Facebook.com/LovetheSAT</u>)!

Quiz #2: Review of Timeless Time Management (p. 50)

1. **A** - Exactly - when you know precisely what you want to DO with your life, you'll naturally be much more skilled at arranging your schedule and your priorities.
2. **D** - Exactly! "Flow" is the state of losing track of time as you work, because you're ENJOYING your work and being CHALLENGED at the same time. The things that put us in flow are big clues to our passions in life.
3. **F** - That's right - daily journal is a great idea for ALL these reasons and more. You'll never know how truly useful it is to keep a journal until you TRY it for 30 days.
4. **C** - Exactly. If you PUSH yourself to stay focused and prohibit distractions, then 90 minutes is the approximate limit to your unbroken focus. Take a break after 90 minutes even if you THINK you can keep going. When you come back to your work recharged after the break you will be MUCH more efficient and focused.
5. **B** - Yup! Obeying "cross-offability" helps prevent endlessly-growing to-do lists and forces you to break down large goals into smaller sub-tasks that can be completed in a reasonable amount of time.
6. **A** - Exactly! It's hard to pin down since everyone needs different amounts of sleep, but 7-10 hours is about right for the majority of us.
7. **B** - Yup! That's exactly who he was, and that's why people love him even to this day ;)
8. **C** - Yup! It's just a saying, but it's one that I've always liked - because I've personally witnessed the possibilities of teaching yourself important lessons by reading the top three books in a field.

How did you do on Quiz #2? Share your results and questions on the Facebook wall (www.Facebook.com/LovetheSAT)!

Quiz #3: Mid-Section Review (p. 107)

1. **C** - Yup! Because of his single-minded focus starting in high school, Sam has been doing quite well in the challenging of movie-making from a young age!
2. **A** - Yes, that sums it up exactly! When you "save" the world you're working hard and when you "savor" the world you're stopping to "actively relax" and enjoy life.
3. **D** - Yes, exactly! Since it's a YEARLY calendar, plan out the biggest events of the YEAR and budget extra time for them in advance. Then fill in the gaps with your smaller monthly, weekly, and daily activities.
4. **E** - Yes! Taking notes is INCREDIBLY effective, but that doesn't mean it's an excuse not listen and contribute. Taking notes is an art and science that takes PRACTICE and experience to be fully effective for each student.
5. **C** - Yes, exactly. CHOOSING and MAKING your own flashcards gets 2x-10x better results than trying to order the "best" flashcards from a big company.
6. **A** - Exactly! Flashcards are the ULTIMATE way to maximize your study time when memorizing specific terms, formulas, and small facts.
7. **A** - Yup! When it comes to being late with assignments, direct honesty and an early warning are your two best options, so use them together. The worst they can say is "NO" and in that case you're no worse off.
8. **C** - Yes - CONTROL is what allows you to DEPEND on always having a great space to do homework. This cuts down on procrastination and greatly reduces overall stress and decision-making each day!
9. **C** - Just so. Technology continues to save us time, but ALSO offer a distractions. Make sure YOU stay in control of your technology, not the other way around!
10. **B** - That's right - although the daily mini-quizzes and small homework assignments don't mean that much on their OWN, it's the overall TREND of those mini-grades that is so important.

How did you do on Quiz #3? Share your results and questions on the Facebook wall (www.Facebook.com/LovetheSAT)!

CHRISTIAN HEATH
Quiz #4: Review of Time Management for High Schoolers (p. 173)

1. **D** - Absolutely right – there's no such thing as starting SAT/ACT prep "too early" in high school. Not only are these tests CRITICAL to your college and scholarship odds, these tests are also HUGE, and you don't want to get caught cramming. It's always easier to review than to learn for the first time – so get started as soon as you can.
2. **C** - Yup! Top students frequently start planning and working on college and scholarship searches and applications up to TWO YEARS before they are due.
3. **C** - Yes, exactly – take your time to think it over, but it's generally a good policy to get OUT of unfilling and useless activities that you're only doing because you think you're "supposed to."
4. **E** - On the balance, peer pressure is mostly a BAD thing that diverts us from our true path, leads us to willingly compromise our principles, and waste time. In general, you should be VERY careful when you feel that you might be bending your personality, wants, or beliefs due to peer pressure.
5. **C** - Yes - this is the biggest risk. It's easy to put your open Algebra II textbook on the table, then sit around talking with friends and having a social hour. And worst of all, your brain will THINK you've been studying more than you actually have!
6. **B** - Yes – 50/50 is pretty close to the IDEAL mix of work and relaxation. The weekend if "free" time - not just "lazy" time, but *also* not just "work" time. Try to get ahead on big projects and goals.
7. **B** - Yes, exactly - my theory is that after being really TIRED from school or work, everyone WANTS to work on their big goals during the holidays - but, they're TOO tired, catching up on rest, relaxation and sleep... and when the vacation ENDS, they suddenly realize they didn't get any closer to their goals... and suddenly they feel BAD about the holiday!
8. **A** - Yes, exactly - motivation and time management are purely INTERNAL, and parents can't force them on teens even if you want to help. Instead, teens should be encouraged and guided to finding their true passions, and good time management will NATURALLY proceed from there.
9. **C** - Yes, my college story was largely about transitioning from an aimless high schooler with no real leadership positions, into a focused, hard-working leader in a field I TRULY cared about and loved (classical piano).

How did you do on Quiz #4? Share your results and questions on the Facebook wall (www.Facebook.com/LovetheSAT)!

190

Quiz #5: Review of the Conclusion (p. 185)

1. **A** - Awesome, thanks for going to the Facebook wall (www.Facebook.com/LovetheSAT) and sharing the number-one thing you learned with me from this book!
2. **A** - Yes - reviewing and summarizing your personal course notes would be the BEST step to take right after you finish the course.
3. **D** - Awesome! I want you to come back as my student - so please enroll TODAY in your next course with me, and order any books you like, from www.LovetheSAT.com!
4. **A** – Excellent! Amazon.com reviews and honest feedback help me AND my business grow. Thank you so much!
5. **F** – Yes! We love having a variety of ways to contact us. Please get in touch any or all ways that work best for you :D

How did you do on Quiz #5? Share your results and questions on the Facebook wall (www.Facebook.com/LovetheSAT)!

ABOUT THE AUTHOR

Christian Heath is a teacher, entrepreneur, musician, and motorcyclist. His tutoring company, Love the SAT Test Prep, has a loyal following and sky-high ratings in Austin, TX.

In addition to creating online courses and writing books for the company, Christian has published hundreds of free articles at his original blog, www.eSATPrepTips.com, and continues to write for www.LovetheSAT.com/blog.

As a musician, Christian once specialized in classical piano, and continues to work on secret projects on the side... His ambitions as a motorcyclist are to explore the world on two wheels - from the highest mountains to the dustiest dirt roads!

He'll see you out there!!!

For More Great Lessons from Christian Heath and Love the SAT Test Prep:

Complete Online Courses for Teens:

- Ultimate Time Management for Teens and Students
  (Get the complete course on discount just for you!)
  - https://www.udemy.com/ultimate-time-management-for-teens-and-high-school-students/?couponCode=TimeBookCompleteCourse

- Conquer SAT Vocabulary for Higher Reading and Verbal Scores
  - https://www.udemy.com/conquer-sat-vocabulary/?couponCode=TimeManagementBook

- Winning College Scholarships for High Schoolers
  - https://www.udemy.com/winning-college-scholarships/?couponCode=TimeBookScholarship

Print Books and eBooks:

Look for them on Amazon.com and LovetheSAT.com!

- SAT Grammar Crammer

- (Coming Soon) Top 30 Incredible Examples for High School Essay Evidence

Free Articles and Blogs:
- www.LovetheSAT.com/blog
- www.eSATPrepTips.com/articles

On Social Media:
- www.Facebook.com/LovetheSAT
- Twitter: @LovetheSAT
- Find us on YouTube!

Web, Email and Phone:
- www.LovetheSAT.com/contact_us
- Help@LovetheSAT.com
- 1-800-653-8994

Made in the USA
San Bernardino, CA
20 September 2018